INTERNET, GOVERNANCE AND DEMOCRACY

D1601233

INTERNET, GOVERNANCE DEMOCRACY

Democratic Transitions from Asian and European Perspectives

Compiled by Jens Hoff

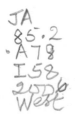

First published in 2006 by NIAS Press
Nordic Institute of Asian Studies
Leifsgade 33, DK–2300 Copenhagen S, Denmark
tel: (+45) 3532 9501 • fax: (+45) 3532 9549
E–mail: books@nias.ku.dk • Website: www.niaspress.dk

British Library Cataloguing in Publication Data
Internet, governance and democracy : democratic transitions from Asian
    and European perspectives. - (Nordic proceedings in Asian studies ;
    no.7)
1.Internet - Political aspects - Asia - Congresses
2.Internet - Political aspects - Denmark - Congresses
3.Democratization - Asia - Congresses 5.Asia - politics and
    government - 1945- - Congresses 6.Denmark - politics and
    government - 1972- - Congresses
I.Hoff, Jens
303.4'833'095

ISBN 87-91114-67-5

Typesetting by Translations ved LJ
Produced by Bookchase
Printed and bound in Great Britain

Contents

Foreword

Information and communication technologies (ICT), in particular the Internet, are technologies that penetrate and affect all societies today. They tie the world together in new ways, and play a major role in the reconfiguration of markets as well as states and civil society. Great hopes have been attached to these technologies; not least concerning their potential to spearhead transitions towards (more) democracy and better governance. The latter concerns are the focus of this book, which explores their potentials in a number of Asian countries as well as Denmark.

Bringing together Asian and Danish researchers to discuss issues related to the Internet and democracy was the central idea behind the conference held on 24 September 2003 at the University of Aalborg in Denmark. The theme was "Democratic Transitions? Will the Internet Bring About More Democracy and Better Governance?" All chapters in this volume originate from presentations at that conference. The conference was a part of the cultural festival "Images of Asia"; a major event held in Denmark in August and September 2003 presenting a massive amount of Asian drama, music, literature, science, etc. to a Danish audience. One of the aims of the festival was to stimulate a dialogue between Asia and Denmark about the role of media in Asia and Denmark. This book is an outcome of that dialogue, and bears witness to its success (see also Bergquist 2004).

Seen from a Danish perspective it was immensely interesting to hear and read about the attempts at using the Internet for democratic purposes; stimulating political participation and empowering citizens and communities, as well as the difficulties encountered, in various Asian countries engaging in such activities. Many of the contributors who live and work in Asian countries present here for the very first time analyses of the political and democratic uses of the Internet in their respective countries. In this sense this volume is really novel and represents a true pioneering effort.

Making such pioneering effort possible is primarily due to the Asian participants, but also the Danish participants at the conference deserve credit for their engaged response. We would therefore like to take this opportunity to thank all participants at the original conference for their contributions to what was an enjoyable event, and an eye-opener for most of us whether coming from Denmark or not. Also, it is pleasing that everyone has taken the pain to rewrite their original presentations in the light of the discussions at the conference, and in a format that has made it possible to print them in this volume.

Finally we will like to thank the sponsors who made the conference possible. These were the Department of Economics, Politics and Public Administration at Aalborg University; The Digital North Denmark; Danish Center for Culture and Development (DCCD); the Center for Research on Media and Democracy in the Network Society (MODINET); the Danish Association for International Co-operation (MS); and the Nordic Institute of Asian Studies(NIAS).

Also warm thanks to Anders Højmark Andersen for his assistance in organizing the conference and to Lene Jakobsen, who took the trouble to linguistically revise, improve and proofread all the chapters in this volume.

Jens Hoff
Professor, Department of Political Science, University of Copenhagen

Jørgen Delman
Director, NIAS – Nordic Institute of Asian Studies

REFERENCES

Bergquist, Karin Bo (ed.), *Images of Asia: Cultural Perspectives on a Changing Asia*, Copenhagen: Danish Center for Culture and Development, 2004

Introduction

JENS HOFF

When I first began writing this introduction, images of the tsunami disaster in Southeast Asia kept appearing and disappearing on my TV screen in an apparently endless stream. Even in a secure haven like Copenhagen, it was difficult not to be deeply moved by the amount of suffering and destruction involved. This feeling was primarily generated by the heartbreaking pictures shown, but it was also due to the fact that even though the disaster hit one continent only, and hit it hard, the victims were from all continents. Hence, apart from the countries directly affected by the tsunami most victims were from Northern Europe; and among these a sizeable number was from Nordic countries. Thus the tsunami was a truly global disaster, as the whole world was affected and the whole world was reacting. Further-more, the disaster was global in scope because mankind was able to communicate about a disaster of such proportions in "real-time". Indeed, the modern means of mass communication – TV, radio and the Internet – were indispensable not only for documenting the size and shape of the disaster but also for creating a global dialogue about it. A dialogue that more than ever before took place on the Internet. TV networks, newspapers and volunteers in many countries created websites that were used by relatives in their search for family members or friends, to create useful contacts, and ask for help from those who had been successful in their search. E-mail was used when public telephone systems became overburdened. In many cases this proved to be a quicker and more reliable way of obtaining information than through public authorities. The Internet also has been used by survivors to tell about their dreadful experiences when the tsunami hit, thus helping them to air their shock and despair. In Denmark it was even possible to see amateur videos of the tsunami strike on the homepage of national public service TV. How oddly it may sound, some have talked about the aftermath of the tsunami as the "the Internet's biggest moment" [1], i.e. the Internet demonstrated some of its potential by helping relieve effects of the disaster.

Thus, in the wake of the tsunami modern information and communication technology, not least the Internet, proved to play a pivotal role in obtaining information about the disaster as well as communicating and discussing it world-wide; a true example of what is meant by globalization. Indeed some call the Internet a frontrunner or an important driver of globalization. The events in South East Asia proved that they might have a point. Hereby the events also demonstrated the raison d'être of this book, which is to show that information and communication technology (ICT)/the Internet are a technologies which penetrates and affects all societies today; a technology which is embraced more or less enthusiastically (often more), and to which great hopes for the future are attached.

The Internet ties the world together in new ways, and helps to reconfigure markets, politics and civil society, likewise the second great theme of this book: democracy. There is no doubt that democracy has become the dominant political norm globally, thus no country, no matter how totalitarian, is unaffected by it [2]. That this is true is evident in most of the chapters of this book, not least the chapters from the different Asian countries, which all are, in one way or another, preoccupied with the interplay between the Internet and democracy and the role played by the Internet in current democratic transitions. Thus, the main concern of in this book is whether the Internet can really be a driving force in a transition towards (more) democracy and better governance, and what contextual conditions are needed in order to redeem the assumed democratic potentials of the Internet. As shall be clear from the case studies unfolded in the following chapters two or three hypotheses constitute cornerstones in the analyses carried out. Some analyses assume that the Internet will bring about more transparency in policy-making and governance, and that it will enhance democratic participation and empower citizens. Others disagree, arguing that no such guarantees exist; rather the Internet is more likely to become a new tool for reinforcement of traditional centers of power and traditional patterns of political behavior and governance relations. Others again, taking care not to become technology determinists, see a democratic outcome of increased Internet use as dependent on a number of contextual factors such as level of economic development, the character of the political system and national as well as trans-national regulatory frameworks, political motivation and political participation of citizens, etc.

A key concern of this book is to provide basic information about Internet usage and democracy in order to make comparisons between Denmark and Asia and between different Asian countries. The comparisons may, given the origin and nature of this book, be rather impressionistic, as the case studies presented are not based on any kind of coherent comparative research methodology. On the other hand the case studies are comprehensive enough to give an idea about Internet usage and diffusion in the countries analysed (Nepal, China, Malaysia, Singapore and Denmark), the difficulties associated with the implementation and uptake of Internet technology in the respective countries, and the attempts of using the Internet in different kinds of democratic practices. Several of the contributions presented here describe for the first time this technology, and the associated democratic ideas and practices from "within", i.e. by researchers who themselves live and carry out research in Asian countries. In this sense this book is a true pioneering effort.

One may ask what is the purpose of bringing case studies from Denmark and Asia together in a book, thereby assuming that comparison is both possible and meaningful? Indeed one may query if the level and diffusion of the implied technology, the democratic tradition and practices, and a host of other contextual factors are too different to make any kind of comparisons feasible. At first glance, the countries represented in this volume apparently present us with what, in the language of comparative research, is known as a "most different case design". A case of point may be comparing Denmark – representing one of the most advanced nations of the world in the terms of Internet diffusion (more than 70% of households have Internet access), "IT-readiness", its well-rooted democracy and politically interested and active citizens – to a country like for example Nepal with an Internet diffusion (number of account holders) of 0.14%, less than 1% of the population using e-mail and Internet and politically the country is beleaguered by a civil war endangering its relatively new and fragile democracy.

However, such gross differences should not overshadow the fact that there also are huge differences within the Asia Pacific region, as well as within the single countries. Thus, countries like Taiwan, South Korea, Hong Kong, Singapore and Japan have high rates of Internet diffusion (more than 50% by end of 2002), and in a country like China Internet access and usage is growing quickly in the bigger cities and among teenagers. A (2003) survey referred to in the chapter by Bu Wei shows that, on average 63% of teenagers are using the Internet to a greater or smaller degree in seven bigger cities, including Beijing. Within the different countries (including Denmark) we also observe huge "digital divides" between regions, between cities and countryside, between rich and poor and between young and old. When we look at political practices and democracy there are also huge differences between the countries in the Asia Pacific region, some being very authoritarian with little room for democratic practices and dissent, while others have or seem to be on the road to a relatively stable parliamentary democracy.

The huge differences between the Asian countries included in this book means that it is difficult to talk about a "most different case design" in its pure form when comparing Denmark to the Asian countries. Nonetheless it still makes sense to compare the impact of ICT/the Internet on ideas and strategies of policy-makers, public administrations and civil society organizations concerning political processes, good governance and democracy. Thus, to the extent that we find similarities and congruent developments between the different countries it points towards the strength of the technology itself (or the uniform thinking about its uses) in bringing about these changes. However, to the extent that we see differences or different developmental paths, it stresses the importance of contextual and country-specific factors.

Looking at all the contributions of this volume we see that they all generally, in one way or another are querying how the perceived new democratic opportunities presented by ICT/the Internet is exploited. Generally, it is also quite remarkable how the Asian researchers are more optimistic compared to the Danish researchers. This might be due to a stronger need among the Asian researchers to search for instruments which can help bring about more democracy in their societies. However, more worrying, it might also be due to the fact that in general experiences with this technology are more plentiful in Denmark, where a number of democratic uses of the Internet have already been tried out and evaluated. These experiences have overall led to more moderate expectations as to the democratic outcomes of the new technology. Also, Danish researchers have, like researchers in other western countries [3] become aware of the limitations of the free development of the Internet inherent in the architecture of the net affected by such things as software patents, copyright legislation and digital rights management systems [4]. Thus, attention in these countries have become very focused on what Deibert [5] has called "commercial censorship" or the limitations imposed on the development of the Internet by commercial actors acting according to market logics. In contrast, the Asian researchers presented in this volume are, probably quite naturally, more preoccupied with the ways in which the state in their respective countries tries to regulate and in quite a few cases even censure the Internet [6]. However, one might wonder whether focusing too narrowly on either one of these evils (commercial or state censorship) might lead to the neglect of the other.

The democratizing potential of the Internet, is normally discussed in terms of a number of "technical properties". Such properties can be formulated in different ways as can be seen in the articles by Banerjee and by Hoff. However, Banerjee and Hoff found that the Internet had some basic features: a) it has a non-hierarchical architecture giving people easier and more equal access to the public sphere(s), b) it allows immediate interaction between participants and "all-to-all" communication, and c) because of its global nature control of information is decentralized and the importance of time and space is diminished. However, these features were only potentially democratizing. Generally, the chapters in this volume demonstrate that the extent of potential redemption seems to depend very much on contextual and country-specific factors, especially the character of the political system, the state of media regulation, the possibilities of developing an adequate technological infrastructure (geographically and economically), the thought and strategies of policy-makers and the political participation and motivation of civil society organizations and citizens in general. Thus, the Internet is not a "magical democratic potion" as claimed in the chapter on Nepal, rather different developmental paths are possible as shown in the chapter on China. There is a choice, and the acknowledgement of such choice by policy makers, administrators, civil society organizations and citizens is extremely important for the future of democracy not only in Asia and Denmark, but also on a global scale.

REFERENCES

[1] The Danish newspaper *Politiken*, December 30th, 2004.

[2] Held, David, *Democracy and the Global Order. From the Modern State to Cosmopolitan Governance*. Cambridge: Polity Press, 1995.

[3] Lessig, Lawrence, *Code and other laws of Cyberspace*. Basic Books: New York, 2000.

[4] See contribution by Jens Hoff in this volume.

[5] Deibert, Ronald J., *Black Code: Censorship, Surveillance and the Militarization of Cyberspace*. Paper prepared for the International Studies Association Conference, Portland, Oregon, USA, February 2003.

[6] See contribution by Indrajit Banerjee in this volume.

CHAPTER 1

E-Democracy in Denmark
Black Clouds on a Blue Sky?
JENS HOFF

INTRODUCTION: HIGH HOPES FOR DEMOCRACY

As early as the 1970s and '80s, utopians – especially of an American variety (Etzioni 1975, Toffler 1981, Naisbitt 1982) – drew a picture of a future democracy in which democratic dialogue and decision-making would take place through modern communication technology. At that time it was especially the appearance and growth of technologies like cable-TV and digital telephones that was seen as paving the road for a renewal of democratic institutions and for more democratic forms of participation.

In the 1990s another outburst of "utopian energy" took place (Ilshammer 1997), this time related to the breakthrough of the Internet and its graphical interface "World Wide Web". Now, a number of authors began to discuss the possibilities for what they called "electronic democracy" or "cyber democracy" (Porter 1995, Rheingold 1993, Hague & Loader 1999). However, a common denominator for the teledemocracy of the 1980s and the cyber democracy of the 1990s was that the point of departure for discussions was most often taken in the technology, or in what it was theoretically possible to achieve with the given technology, not (or only to a limited degree) taking existing political institutions, traditions and cultures into consideration.

But what are the technological features of the Internet that conditioned such optimism? According to many authors (van de Donk et al. (eds.) 1995, Hoff, Löfgren & Johansson 1999) there are at least seven properties worth paying attention to:

- *Increased interaction between participants*: compared to traditional mass media (newspapers, TV or radio) the new technology contains the possibility of interactivity between sender and receiver of a message. Typical examples are mailing lists, debate forums and chat sites.

- *The declining importance of time and space*: with the Internet it is possible to access for example the homepages of political organizations or to participate in virtual political debates around-the-clock. Also, territorial boundaries become less important as it is possible to access information and engage in dialogue on a global scale.

- *Easier and more equal access to the public sphere*: compared to traditional mass media the possibilities for "ordinary people" to reach a large audience has been significantly enlarged with Internet technology. It is relatively easy and cheap to create a homepage and in this way share one's ideas with other people without the censorship of (state-owned or commercial) TV, radio and newspapers. Also, virtual communication is more egalitarian than face-to-face communication as participants do not have to reveal for example their gender, age, ethnicity or social position.

- *"All-to-all" communication*: in contrast to traditional mass media, which are based on the "one-to-all" principle, the Internet creates an environment for "all-to-all" communication.

- *Easier access to and control over large amounts of information*: compared to paper-based information, modern information and communication technology (ICT) makes it much easier to find, store and organize huge amounts of information, thus potentially giving the user of such information greater knowledge and oversight capacity than before.

- *Possibilities for both "broadcasting" and "narrowcasting"*: while the Internet is well suited for "all-to-all" communication it is also possible to use it in a more narrow way to either target special groups or to maintain discussions among such groups.

- *Decentralization of control with information*: in contrast to traditional mass media where the control of information is in the hands of state owned or commercial TV companies or multinational media networks, ICT gives the individual citizen and all types of organizations the possibility of becoming their own editor and publisher, potentially able to reach a global audience.

Thus the new ICTs, especially the Internet, seemed to create a new political opportunity structure – "affordance" in the word of Hutchby 2003 – shifting power away from governments and media monopolies towards citizens and social movements, and at the same time laying a foundation for a more transparent and participatory polity. This impression was underpinned by the virtual presence of a steeply increasing number of organizations of all kinds, some of them especially concerned with democracy and the Internet (e.g. Minnesota E-democracy, the WELL, UK citizens online), and associated or freestanding debate forums. Also, the democratic character of the Internet was stressed by the accounts of how the Net had successfully been used by suppressed groups like the Zapatistas[1] in Mexico or the Chechen liberation movement in Russia to inform about and create global support for their cause; and to circumvent state-controlled media (for example in China in relation to the events on the Tiananmen Square, or in Russia in relation to Yeltsin's coming to power). Furthermore the democratic potential of ICTs was stressed in national ICT plans like "Infosamfundet 2000" (The Information Society, Year 2000; published in 1994) and successor "Det Digitale Danmark – omstilling til netværkssamfundet" (Digital Denmark – Transformation to the Network Society, 1999), comprising the plans of the Danish Government. Together, all these developments served to cement a myth about the inherent democratic character of ICT. Thus, the more the possibilities of the technology could be unfolded, and the more that PCs and the Internet could be spread to all corners of society, the more democracy would prevail.

This late 1990s discourse on the Internet and democracy led the Danish author Tor Nørretranders to call the Internet: "a successful piece of anarchy" (Nørretranders 1997:7); the Internet was widely seen as an open, free and liberal public sphere and agora. However, the advent of the millenium seems to have changed all that. Thus, with the growing economic

---

1. Castells (1997:68ff) even calls the Zapatistas the "First Informational Guerilla Movement".

and political importance of the Internet, it has increasingly become the object of different kinds of regulation and control, and especially since 9/11 there has been a dramatic growth in what the Canadian IT researcher Ronald Deibert (2003) has called state and commercial censorship.

In Denmark, state censorship of the Internet has been unknown until recently. However, with a letter from the Minister of Justice Lene Espersen to municipalities and counties commanding their public libraries to install filters on their Internet-connected computers (notably to prevent citizens from surfing for websites with a pedophilic content), a first step in that direction was taken in August 2003 (see www.dbf.dk/default.asp?ID=1084). Concerning so-called commercial censorship, recent developments within the patent area mean that the possibilities of patenting software have been greatly enlarged. Together with the digital rights management systems being built into among others the next generation of Windows, which structure media communication in significant ways, this will enhance the monopolistic powers of the big hardware and software companies; a company like Microsoft will be constituted as a new political authority able to dominate considerable parts of the global communications infrastructure.

Below I shall discuss this first Danish step towards state censorship by looking at the effects of the known filtering technologies. Secondly, I shall look at what commercial censorship means for different aspects of democracy, and finally I shall look at some countervailing evidence: an example of a successful democratic experiment in a Danish municipality.

STATE CENSORSHIP IN DENMARK?

As mentioned, Deibert (2003) points to the fact that the Internet has increasingly become the object of state and commercial censorship. Actually, he points to three set of actors who are struggling to control the Internet in a complicated form of governance: the nation states (and the EU); big multinational hardware, software and telecommunications companies and media conglomerates; and civic networks/NGO's which specifically aim at influencing the global communications policy (e.g. Association for Progressive Communications, Computer Professionals for

Social Responsibility, Human Rights Watch, Reporters Without Borders). To this should be added two more sets of actors.

First are a couple of private, non-profit organizations that have been licensed to control (or set themselves up to build) specific features of the Internet. Most notable here is ICANN (the Internet Corporation for Assigned Names and Numbers), established in 1998, an organization that coordinates the assignment of Internet domain-names, IP-addresses and protocol parameters. The organization is also in charge of coordinating the maintenance of the Internets backbone server architecture. Another important organization is W3C (World Wide Web Consortium), which develops inter-operative technologies (specifications, guidelines, software, etc.) meant to further the technological development of the Internet. The W3C-team is lead by Tim Berners-Lee, who is regarded as the "inventor" of the Internet.

Second, the United Nations has recently become a player in this field through its arrangement of the first World Summit of Information Technology (WSIS) held in Geneva in June 2003 (based on UN resolution 56/183). The main aim of the UN involvement in the field is to find means to bridge the digital divide between North and South, and to find ways to create access to the global information infrastructure for the peoples of less developed countries. To reach this goal the collaboration of governments, civil society, business and international organizations is sought, and at the moment a series of so-called PrepCom (Preparatory Committee) conferences are taking place in order to finalize the WSIS Declaration of Principles and Plan of Action (see www.wsis.org or www.una.dk/wsis).

Focusing first on state censorship, it is well known that many totalitarian regimes censor Internet content by installing filters at the server level to control users' access. In a 1999 report from Freedom House, a free speech organization, 45 countries were identified as censuring Internet content among these Azerbaijan, Cuba, China, North Korea, Iran, Iraq, Saudi Arabia, Syria and Vietnam (see Staksrud 2002).

However, the use of filters and filtering techniques is only one out of a number of ways in which nation states try to regulate the Internet. Other strategies are: 1) laws regulating this new area of mass communication, 2) self- or co-regulation by/with the Internet industry through the use of commonly agreed ethical rules, 3) use of hotlines to fight especially pedophilic content, and 4) information campaigns. Here I will focus on the question of filters and filtering techniques, as this is what is currently at stake in Denmark. The point of departure for the discussion will be filters developed in the US, as they dominate the market today.

Generally one can say that what filtering programs do is that they compare parts of or a whole data-file (for example a newsgroup, a document or a website) with a pre-defined set of rules. The result of the comparison determines whether the user will be allowed to receive and view the file on his/her computer. Common rules for filtering are:

- Blocking of certain files or websites by comparing their URL, name or IP-address with a list of forbidden files or websites (blacklisting)

- Blocking all files except already accepted files or websites (white listing)

- Filtering of chosen files/websites by comparing their content with a list of words, word combinations or other identifiable elements (for example degree of nakedness)

- Filtering of chosen files/websites by comparing a classification mark associated with the file/website with a predefined set of classification criteria.

The two first types of blocking require that a person has evaluated each file/website and decided whether it should be either black- or white-listed. The third type of filtering requires that a person defines the list of forbidden words or word combinations, but the selection itself is automatic. The last form of blocking demands that a person establishes classification criteria and then marks every file and website. After marking, the files/websites can be filtered according to given criteria. The classification takes place through the content providers or a third party, for example a government body, and is a prerequisite for many filtering programs.

Some of the best known filtering programs are Cyberpatrol, CYBERsitter, Net Nanny, SurfWatch, BAIR and Safesurf. However, it has been disclosed by among others Peacefire, an organization fighting for children and youngsters right to information and freedom of speech, that all of these market-leading filters have blocked information that should not have been blocked according to their own rules. Thus, Cyberpatrol has blocked student organizations at certain American universities and UseNet discussion groups like alt.journalism and soc.feminism. for a considerable amount of time blocked Cyber Patrol also the Electronic Frontier Foundation and HotWired. Also, the organization Planned Parenthood is blocked. Net Nanny blocks newsgroups with information about AIDS plus women organizations and equal rights organizations like soc.feminism, alt.feminism and the National Organization for Women in the USA. Furthermore it has been documented that during the elections in the USA in 2000, a number of candidates – both Democrats and Republicans – had their websites blocked by CyberPatrol.

Elisabeth Staksrud (2002), in her article from where I have most of the above information on commercial filters, concludes that as the known filters have such obvious errors, they risk making matters worse than before. Firstly, by creating a false sense of security, as one is led to believe that children and youngsters are protected by these filters. Secondly, because important value choices are made by the producers of the filters. When women organization, some politicians and proponents for free speech are blocked, this is a form of political censorship being imposed on an audience with little knowledge of what is going on.

Thus, when the Danish Minister of Justice tries to force public libraries to install filters on their Internet-connected computers in order to prevent citizens from surfing for websites with a pedophilic content, this is a policy which is not only likely to be quite ineffective with the known filtering technologies, but also a policy which is likely to limit access to information and legitimate expressions of free speech. It is a type of symbolic control policy, which is harmful to democracy. It is, however, sadly in line with policies in the USA demanding the use of commercial filters in schools and public offices (Staksrud 2002:77).

COMMERCIAL CENSORSHIP

With the concept "commercial censorship" Deibert (2003) denotes the different ways in which commercial actors try to influence and dominate the Internet. In our kind of societies most of these practices are of course 100 per cent legitimate and normal. However, as I shall try to illustrate, a number of existing and especially emerging practices seem to have properties that impinge on issues like access (in the broadest sense), privacy, diversity and openness in a negative way, thereby undermining important aspects of democracy.

There are at least five strategies that commercial actors use in trying to maximize their profits when dealing with ICT, in particular the Internet: 1) to become market leaders set this de facto standards; examples are Microsoft (Office, Internet Explorer), Oracle (databases) and Adobe (pdf-files), 2) work in international standards organizations to set de jure standards (CEN, ETSI, IEC, 3)[2] to take out patents (on hardware, software), 4) to register copyright on their products, and 5) to ensure copyright protection by de-veloping digital rights management systems.

Here I shall deal only with recent developments within the copyright and copyright protection area, and the software patent area, as it is especially developments within these areas that are of democratic concern at the moment.

Concerning copyright we know that with the digitalization of a wide range of consumer products (including movies, music and books), pirate duplication and distribution has become a problem. Companies in the affected industries such as the recording industry and the motion picture industry have claimed large losses in potential sales, even though determining exact figures is very difficult. It is therefore not surprising that the involved companies and their associations such as the RIAA (Recording Industry Association of America) and the MPAA (Motion Picture Association of America) have taken increasingly stronger measures to protect their property and preserve copyright in cyberspace. Naturally, there are good reasons to support copyright measures because without a system to protect against theft and plagiarism and to ensure appropriate compensation for expended resources, the circulation of ideas central to liberal democratic society could wither. However, the problem seems to be that in cyberspace it is difficult in practice to apply the longstanding principles of protection of intellectual property, and that the measures taken

---

2.   CEN is an acronym for European Committee for Standardization, ETSI is an acronym for European Telecommunications Standards Institute, and IEC is the International Electrotechnical Commission.

seem to have a number of unintended consequences, among these restrictions on creativity and self-expression. Most bothersome from a democratic perspective is, however, the development of so-called digital rights management (DRM), systems which work on the basis of codes built directly into the communications media themselves (for example into the motherboard of PCs).

If we look first at one notorious example of copyright protection, the Digital Millenium Copyright Act, an act passed by US Congress on 28 October 1998, it has been shown in a study by the Electronic Frontier Foundation that the Act has been employed as an anti-competitive tool, that it has stifled legitimate research into cyber-security and encryption technologies, and that is has undermined "fair use" of products. It has also impinged on academic databases and electronic journals restricting their use, and many believe that the Act will put restrictions on academic work in the public domain (see www.law.duke.edu/pd/papers.html#history).

We could console ourselves with the fact that the Digital Millenium Copyright Act (DMCA) is only an American law if it was not for the fact that similar heavy-handed laws are being adopted in a number of other countries. Also, the US is pushing the DMCA in bilateral trade negotiations, and many of its elements are manifest in treaties administered by the World Intellectual Property Organization (WIPO).

However, of greater concern from a democratic point of view are the measures currently being taken to protect intellectual property and copyright through technical means; in particular the attempts to build codes into software and hardware to structure permissible communications. Most notable in this respect is Microsoft's Palladium system and the work going on in the so-called Trusted Computing Software Alliance (TCPA); an organization set up by Intel, IBM, Microsoft, HP and Compaq, but which today comprises more than 100 IT-firms.

Palladium[3] is a further development of Microsoft's existing DRM system, which works with sound and video files in Microsoft's Media Player. A recoding company or a video producer who wishes to control the use and copying of the product on the buyer's computer can use Microsoft's Media Player. With software

---

3. 'The following information on Microsoft's Palladium system is all from Bjerke (2003).

from Microsoft the producer can change the sound or video files to encrypted files, which can only run on Media Player if the user has a digital key, something the user has to buy. The producer can regulate the number of times a tune can be listened to or a video can be shown, and whether the sound or video file can be copied or burnt on a CD. This system is very similar to other DRM systems, also those developed on open source platforms. However, a major difference is that Palladium generalizes the DRM system, so that the whole operating system on a given PC will be controlled by a system of rights, where not only sound or video files but also e-mail, databases, text, pictures and other programs are protected against unauthorized use.

If things turn out as Microsoft expects, Palladium will become the standard operating system on the next generation of computers. Seen in the context of the market dominance of central Microsoft products like the Office package and Internet Explorer, Microsoft will be able to decide which programs it is possible to run together with its dominating products. If Microsoft programs are used on most people's computers it means that Microsoft will obtain the possibility of denying other programs access to data protected by Microsoft programs. Thus, Microsoft will have a crucial influence on which programs it will be possible to run on the computers. If, therefore, the most important information/content providers in society accept Palladium, it forces citizens to also use Palladium if they want to buy text, sound, or video files, or if they want to send and receive protected e-mails and other information from (for example) public authorities. Microsoft claims that one of Palladiums big advantages is that the user can avoid viruses etc. because only accepted programs can run under Palladium. However, the same functionality can be obtained by IBM's TCPA-system for Linux. The crucial difference is that while IBM gives the owner of the PC a possibility to protect himself against "foreign" attempts to change the software on the computer, Microsoft is protecting the "foreign" content providers against the owner if he/she attempts at making changes to his/hers PC.

That this is not a technological fairy tale is evident by the WIPO and EPO[4] patent applications sent in by Microsoft in order to patent their DRM and TCPA

---

4.   WIPO is the World Intellectual Property Organization, and EPO is the European Patent Office.

systems. In December 2001 Microsoft obtained a US patent on a "Digital Rights Management Operating System", which is likely to be used to block competing DRM operating systems, safeguarding Microsoft's position as the only provider of DRM systems.

Thus, the coming of DRM systems should be seen in connection with the development in the area of software patents, and it is exactly the combined development that makes the situation very problematic from a democratic point of view.

To cut a long story very short there has for some time been a big difference in the American and the European approach to software patents. Whereas it has not been possible to patent software in either Denmark or the rest of Europe, software patenting has been possible in the USA. However, the EPO has now changed its practice and made a reinterpretation of the European Patent Convention so that it is possible to patent most software that can be run on a computer (given that it is new, and can be characterized as an "invention").

To make matters worse a new EU Directive, which is being negotiated in the European Parliament at this very moment (September 2003), will force the EU countries to pass legislation that widens the field for software patents even more than the new practice of the EPO. If the Directive is passed this will bring the European situation very close to conditions in the USA.[5]

But what is wrong with software patents? Isn't it just a legitimate compensation for the costs of developing new products, and isn't the reward of a patent a necessary incentive for innovation? This is a long discussion which is a outside the scope of this paper, but a number of authors - among them Hart, Holmes and Reid (2001), and Bjerke (2003) - has convincingly shown that software is a special type of product, the patenting of which will have a number of negative consequences. Firstly, software patents seem to primarily protect the market position of dominating firms more than

---

5.   Concerning the EU Directive on Software Patents the thrust of the directive was changed through a very active intervention by the open source movement in a number of European countries. The directive now states that it is only possible to patent software that steers hardware use, but that all other types of software cannot be patented. However, the directive still need to pass the Ministerial Council, and might therefore still be subject to buy watering down. Also, the practice of the EPO has become very lax in this field, probably due to pressure from big business.

stimulating innovation. Secondly, institutions – also public institutions – will loose the right to know about what is going on in their IT infrastructure as most of the programs they will be using will have hidden code. Thirdly, access to the Internet and other forms of digital exchange of information requires common standards. With the new patent regime it will be possible to patent such standards. If this happens paying a fee to use the Internet is a very likely prospect. Also, this can mean that it will be difficult to protect oneself against possible secret tapping of information.

Returning to the next generation of Windows (the Palladium system) again, through the combination of patented Microsoft standards, and the dominance of Microsoft programs on many citizens' computers, Microsoft is likely to get a crucial influence on the type of programs required to read much of the information on the Internet. A worst-case scenario is that even search engines will have to be certified by Microsoft before citizens can make use of them. In this way Microsoft and its partners will obtain a crucial power to decide about what it is possible to distribute over the Net and what not – a power which is very reminiscent of a censuring function. Also, Microsoft will be able to tap computers for information, and this goes for citizens, businesses and public authorities. This seems in itself to be reason enough to seriously reconsider the pending EU Directive on software patents, and to make sure that open source alternatives to Palladium exist. It is true of course, that citizens, businesses and public authorities will get better possibilities of controlling their internal communication with Palladium, and be able better to avoid hacking etc. But insofar as it will be Microsoft who is checking the fundamental identity of both hardware and software, citizens will have to get this identity certified regularly by Microsoft. In fact, this is already happening today with Windows XP (Jennings 2003). This creates a way for Microsoft to access people's data. As even the information activities of criminals and terrorists will be protected by Palladium, both police and intelligence services will be likely to try to obtain information through collaboration with Microsoft.

Thus, by way of a conclusion we can say that if Microsoft gets away with patenting Palladium, this will give Microsoft power of enormous dimensions - a legislative power (control over programs and access to information), judicial (it will judge about violations), and an executive power (it can block access to information) - in a world where computers and the Internet, at least in the rich part of the world, are increasingly the means of citizens' access to news, entertainment, information, products of various kinds, jobs, private communication, etc. This power, which is furthermore highly automated, will set Microsoft up as a very significant political authority in the information society.

Summing up, concerning these examples of state and commercial censorship what we see is a serious undermining of the Internet as an open, liberal and free public arena. Gradually limitations on access in the widest sense as both free access to different kinds of hardware/software and information, on privacy, on diversity and on openness have been or is being imposed. This infringement on the Internet as a symbol of liberal democracy is happening in the shadow of "the war on terrorism", and the Internet might be seen as one of the bigger casualties of this war.

IS THERE STILL HOPE FOR DEMOCRACY? : A LOCAL DANISH EXPERIENCE

Deibert (2003), in the article referred to a couple of times above, also paints a very bleak picture of the possibilities of using the Internet for civic democratic communications, and of its becoming a truly democratizing force. However, he sees some hope in the forces that are currently fighting censorship and surveillance on the Internet, forces that he identifies as civic networks. Some of these are well known such as the APC (Association for Progressive Communications), Human Rights Watch and Reporters Without Borders. He also seems to invest some hope in progressive elements in the hacker community, for example an activist group like Hactivismo.

While Deibert is basically referring to a North American context, the situation might be somewhat different in Europe. In some EU countries like France and Germany it is becoming official policy to reduce the dependence on Microsoft products. In Germany, 20 per cent of the public administration has now migrated to open source products, and the German Ministry of the Interior has developed a migration plan that all public institutions can follow. Also the EU is devoting considerable sums of money to develop open source products in its 6th Framework Program. (It is ironic of course that this runs counter to the policy resulting from the pending directive on software patents, and maybe even more from the practice of EPO see footnote5). Furthermore, in quite a lot of EU countries political/public institutions have tried to employ ICT for democratic purposes, and some of these experiments and products being supported by the EU. In Denmark such experiments and developments have especially taken place at the municipal level.

Here I am going to refer to what I consider a particularly successful case, namely the case of the so-called OdderWeb developed in the municipality of Odder. Odder is an average sizeed Danish municipality with around 20,000 inhabitants located in Eastern Jutland just south of Aarhus, the second largest Danish city. Its citizens' income and education levels are a little above the national average. Internet diffusion in the municipality is high, and believed to be above the national average of 70 per cent of households (77 per cent including home and work, according to figures for first 6 months of 2003; see Danmarks Statistik 2003. Exact figures for Odder are not known). The municipality has been one of the most ambitious municipalities in Denmark in trying to develop ICT solutions for both administrative and democratic purposes, and the official website of the municipality has been rated among the top five in Denmark for two consecutive years in the annual "Best on the Net" ratings done by the national Board of IT and Telecommunications.

The website of the municipality (www.odder.dk) is a neat and orderly one with information about municipal activities, culture, children and youngsters, education, health and care, housing, tourism, business opportunities, jobs, shopping, etc. It carries interactive services such as a debate forum, possibilities for contacting municipal politicians, for complaining to municipal authorities, for participating in nationwide debates, etc. It also has some transaction services such as "E-boks" (a personal archive for official, electronic documents, bank statements, etc.), the possibility for electronically changing to another physician, the possibility of electronic payment of municipal bills, etc.

However, most interesting from a democratic point of view is probably the so-called OdderWeb, which is an application developed by the small local IT firm Kubus Clevernet Aps. OdderWeb is accessible from/

integrated with the municipal website but its unique characteristic is that it functions as a "private room" on the Internet, a dynamic and easy-to-use website which is accessible only with a private "key" (login). However, once opened one can decide to make the whole website, or parts of it, accessible for everyone. On the website one can upload family pictures, shopping lists, e-mail addresses, enter events in a calendar, keep a log, etc.; functions which can be accessed from anywhere on the Net. However, apart from this "private room" it is also possible to create groups or communities on the website with friends, fellow joggers, to create a virtual classroom with you schoolmates and teachers, etc. The integration with the municipal website also means that you can subscribe to different types of news from the municipality, and have them arrive directly in your own electronic mailbox. Thus, the unique feature of OdderWeb is that it integrates functions for private use, for citizen-to-citizen (C2C) communication, and for citizen-to-administration (C2A) interaction in one web application. The thinking behind the application, stated when of OdderWeb was announced on 25 February 2003, is that by offering citizens an easy-to-use "private space" on the Internet, the municipality will stimulate citizen interest in using the Net, and at the same time improve citizens' proficiency in ICT. This is thought to lead also to an increased use of ICT in interactions with the municipality; thereby enhancing both efficiency and democracy in the municipality.

Concerning the democratic effects, at the launch of OdderWeb, the author was invited to present a proactive evaluation of the possible democratic effects of the application. In so doing I used 10 criteria for a (normative) democratic evaluation of digital applications for political communication developed in Hoff (2000) and in Hoff, Löfgren and Johansson (1999). These criteria are derived from a more traditional view on democracy, as a "parliamentary chain of steering" (the Whitehall-model), as well as from a view that recognizes the tendencial shift in our societies in the direction of governance (March and Olsen 1995). The 10 criteria are:

1) ability for citizens to influence politically (strengthening/weakening)

2) stimulation of public debate in relation to political decision (positive/ negative effect)

3)   whether the municipal boards' capacity to act is increased or not

4)   whether the responsibility and accountability of the municipal board is increased or not

5)   whether the responsibility and accountability of the municipal administration is increased or not

6)   whether citizens become more politically active and responsible

7)   whether there is a positive development in citizens' democratic identities

8)   whether there is a positive development of citizens' political resources and competencies

9)   whether we see a development of relevant narratives on policies and politics (positive stories of possibilities for political community, influence, change, etc.)

10) whether the local political system becomes more flexible in its approach to citizens' wants.

In my proactive evaluation I judged OdderWeb to have a possible positive impact on 5-6 of these dimensions, and none or an uncertain (but not negative) impact on the other 4 dimensions. Thus, OdderWeb was estimated to have a positive impact on dimensions no. 6 to 10, and a more uncertain positive impact on criteria no. 2 (public debate). So according to this (some might say) raw and premature judgement, success was inscribed in OdderWeb from the beginning. And indeed, within some months more than 800 citizens had established their "private room" on OdderWeb equaling around 10 per cent of households with Internet access in Odder.

However, given the global developments described above one might wonder how long the democratic idyll in Odder, as well as elsewhere, might last. What happens to the C2C and C2A networks and communication/ transactions if and when Palladium hits Odder? Will the municipality be able to continue to provide for users of open source software? If not, who will be included and who excluded from this part of the local political community? And what will the municipality do about that? These are just some of the questions that springs to mind – questions of a character that we will increasingly be confronted with in the near future.

CONCLUSION

There are two important lessons to be learned from the analysis above of state and commercial censorship, and of the democratic experiment with ICT at the municipal level in Denmark referred to. The first one is that it is becoming increasingly impossible to separate local and global developments especially in relation to ICT. This of course is what globalization is all about, but the developments described above illustrates very clearly that this is also the case when it comes to politics. As Deibert says: "From now on it is all world domestic politics" (2003:1). Therefore, work for use of the Internet to improve local democracy has to be connected with the work to avoid both state and commercial censorship on a national and a global scale. If not, we risk seeing that both freedom of information (i.e. the right to inform, and to be informed) and personal control over one's own computer (privacy) are seriously diminished.

The second lesson to be learned is that the architecture of the Internet should not be taken for granted. This point has been put forward forcefully by Lawrence Lessig (2000), but today it is clearer than ever before that politicians, public employees, citizens and social scientists can no longer refrain from dealing with so-called "technical issues" as such issues are of enormous economic and political importance. Also, computer scientists, system administrators as well as hard-and software companies can no longer avoid taking ethical and political standpoints on how they want to see their technology being used, and who it is should benefit.

REFERENCES

Bjerke, F. (2003) "Softwarepatenter og magt" in Hoff, J. (ed.): Danmark som informationssamfund. Muligheder og barrierer for politik og demokrati. Aarhus, Aarhus Universitetsforlag

Castells, M. (1997) The Power of Identity. Massachusetts & Oxford, Blackwell Publishers.

Danmarks Statistik (2003) Informationssamfundet Danmark 2003. Copenhagen.

www.dst.dk/pukora/epub/upload/5425/kapitel3.pdf

Deibert, R. (2003) Black Code: Censorship, Surveillance, and the Militarization of Cyberspace. Paper prepared for the International Studies Association Conference, Portland, Oregon, USA. February 2003.

Etzioni, A. (1972) "Minerva. An Electronic Town hall" in Policy Sciences: 3, pp. 457-474.

Forskningsministeriet (1994) "Info-samfundet år 2000. Rapport fra udvalget om Informationssamfundet år 2000." Copenhagen.

Forskningsministeriet (1999): "Det digitale Danmark – omstilling til netværkssamfundet."

http://www.detdigitaledanmark.dk/rapport/ddd.pdf

Hague, B. & Loader, B. (1999)(eds.) Digital Democracy. London & New York, Routledge.

Hart, Holmes & Reid (2001) "The Economic Impact of Patentability of Computer Programs."

http://europa.eu.int/comm/internal_market/en/indprop/comp/studyintro.htm

Hoff, J., Löfgren, K. & S. Johansson (1999) Internet og demokrati. Erfaringer fra kommunalvalget 1997. Jurist- og Økonomforbundets Forlag.

Hoff, J. (2000) "Technology and social change: the path between technological determinism, social constructivism and new institutionalism" in Hoff, J. Horrocks, I. & P. Tops (eds.) Democratic Governance and New Technology. Technologically mediated innovations in political practice in Western Europe. London, Routledge.

Ilshammer,L. (1997) Demokr@ti - det elektroniske folkstyrets möjligheter och problem. (SOU 1997:23). Justitiedepartementet, Stockholm, Fritzes Forlag.

Jennings, M. (2003) "Windows XP Shows the Direction Microsoft is Going" http://www.hevanet.com/peace/microsoft.htm

Lessig, L. (2000) Code and other laws of Cyberspace. New York, Basic Books.

March, J.G. & Olsen, J.P. (1995) Democratic Governance. New York, The Free Press.

Naisbitt, J. (1982) Megatrends: Ten New Directions Transforming Our Lives. New York, Warner Books.

Nørretranders, T. (1997) Stedet som ikke er – Fremtidens nærvær, netværk og Internet. Copenhagen, Aschenhoug.

Porter, M. (1995) " Cyberdemocracy: The Internet and the Public Sphere" in Holmes, D. (ed.): Virtual Politics: Identity and Community in Cyberspace. Whiltshire, Sage Publications.

Rheingold, H. (1993) "A Slice of Life in My Virtual Community" in Harasim, L.M. (ed.): Global Networks – Computers and International Communication. Cambridge, Mass, MIT Press.

Staksrud, E. (2002) "Ytringsfrihet og sensur på Internett. Politisk regulering og kommersiell filtrering" in T. Slaata (eds.): Digital makt. Informasjons- og kommunikasjonsteknologiens betydning og muligheter. Oslo, Gyldendal Norsk forlag: pp.64- 94.

Toffler, A. (1981)(orig. 1980) Den tredje bølge. Copenhagen, Erichsen.

Van de Donk, W.B.H.J. et al. (eds.)(1995) Orwell in Athens: A Perspective on Informatization and Democracy. Amsterdam , IOS Press.

INTERNET RESOURCES

Dansk Biblioteksforening www.dbf.dk/default.asp?ID=1084

World Summit on Information Technology: www.wsis.org

- Danish information on WSIS: www.una.dk/wsis

CHAPTER 2

Political Participation and Democratization
The Role of the Internet in Asia

DR. INDRAJIT BANERJEE

INTRODUCTION

The advent of the Internet has given rise to promises of democratic reali-zation and fulfillment all over the world. The Internet has been regarded as a par-ticularly potent instrument of democratization in countries where the mass media have been controlled by governments thus restricting political debate and participation. It has been argued by nume-rous scholars that the Internet offers new and unprecedented means for information access and dissemination, which are regarded as critical to full political participation by the citizens. The Internet has evolved to become a central component in liberal individualist visions of electronic democracy (Kalathil and Boas, 2003).

Since the 1980s, teledemocracy gurus such as Naisbett (1982), Masuda (1981), Toffler (1981) and others have popularized the notion that the electronic media can be used to facilitate more direct and equitable participation in politics. Since its earliest incarnations, teledemocracy has emphasized the transformational power of electronic communications to empower individuals by providing them with the ability to participate directly in decision-making and governance. Teledemocrats used the 'electronic town meetings and televoting' using cable television systems and telephone as early examples of their vision of the transformation of political participation. The emergence of computer networks and the Internet have enhanced these utopian views of the proponents of teledemocracy leading them to pronounce prophetic visions of push-button digital democracy (Dutton, 1992).

The 1990s have produced a growing body of literature on the impact and implications of the Internet on democratization and governance, however, as this study aims to show, many of these studies have essentially extra-polated the democratizing properties of the Internet from its technical characteristics. Kalathil and Boas highlight some of the key weaknesses of a significant body of recent literature on the political impact of the Internet:

> *First, it often imputes a political character to the Internet itself, rather than focusing on specific uses of the technology. The Internet, however, is only a set of connections between computers (or a set of protocols allowing computers to exchange information); it can have no impact apart from its use by human beings. The conventional wisdom also tends to be based on a series of "black-box" assertions that obscure the ways in which the use of technology might truly produce a political outcome...Subsequent assertions about the technology's political effects are usually made without consideration of the full national context in which the Internet operates in any given country.*(Kalathil and Boas 2003:3)

Seen from the Asian perspective, one of the problems of this growing literature is the fact that an overwhelming majority of studies conducted on the topic of the Internet's potential impact on democratization has taken place in North America and Western Europe, where democratic traditions have been strongly entrenched for centuries (Dahlberg, 2001). Few of these studies therefore assess the democratic use and potential of the Internet in countries that are still in their democratic infancy or are subjugated by authoritarian or semi-authoritarian states.

In Asia, most nations were formed after long periods of colonial rule. In most countries democracy has emerged only after the establishment of political independence and sovereignty in the late 1940s and 1950s. Asian nations can thus be considered generally as fledgling democracies and the advent of the Internet definitely has varying possibilities and implications on the polity of these nations. Only recently have some studies begun to examine the political impact of the Internet on Asian nations (Banerjee, 2003; Ho, Kluver and Yang, 2003, Kalathil and Boas, 2003). These are the first concrete attempts to map the role, use and impact of the Internet on political participation and democratization in Asia.

This paper is inspired by the contention that most studies on the democratic potential of the Internet reveal significant theoretical gaps and recent experiences of the political impact of the Internet in Asia cannot be understood without a thorough contextualization of the analysis. Models of democracy vary from country to country, and the same can be said of political culture, attitudes, and practices. The actual and effective use of the Internet by individuals, groups and political parties is a key determinant of the real impact that the medium can have on political processes and outcomes.

Many of the studies conducted in the past had one major deficiency, making generalizations on the political impact of the Internet based on technical and architectural features of the Internet alone thereby making almost total abstraction and de-contextualization of the national and political contexts in which the Internet was introduced. Mosco (1989) summarizes succinctly the weaknesses of these technological determinist paradigms by arguing that technologies embody, in their production, distribution and use, existing political and social relationships. Technologies therefore are little more than congealed social relationships.

No technology has uniform and undifferentiated effects across countries and contexts. Recent experiences in the political use of the Internet in several Asian countries such as Malaysia, Singapore, China, India and others reveal hitherto unforeseen dynamics that have not been captured by the existing body of literature and theory so far. There is thus a real and urgent need to embed research in this area into the national political context and understand the Internet's use and impact through an approach that takes into account the numerous socio-political factors and variables that intervene in the political use of the Internet. Political systems, democratic models, technological infrastructure, socio-economic development as well as censorship and regulation are some of these context-specific factors which have a key influence on the effective use of the Internet for political empowerment, participation and democracy.

This paper sets out to modestly chart out certain new theoretical avenues that could enhance the understanding of the political uses and impact of the Internet in Asia. These exploratory perspectives aim to highlight the weaknesses of some of the key assumptions of past studies in this area as well as to develop, through an observation of Asian experiences and uses of the Internet in politics, a framework for understanding the ways in which the Internet has been used in the political sphere.

Beginning with an overview of the key assumptions on the Internet's democratic potential, this paper will develop a theoretical critique by presenting the variations in democratic models and practices, the differential and differentiated relation between democracy and information within these models and identify as well as discuss certain key factors that have influenced the political use of the Internet in several Asian countries.

ASSESSING THE INTERNET'S POLITICAL IMPACT: WHAT DO WE KNOW SO FAR?

There is a growing consensus among scholars and politicians around the world that the Internet offers new and unprecedented opportunities to enhance democracy by facilitating public debate and political participation (Kalathil and Boas, 2001). The global and dramatic expansion of the Internet has led to predictions that the Internet will completely break down political control and pose a threat to all authoritarian regimes.

The key argument put forward by most scholars seems to be that the Internet helps set the political agenda and influences, to some extent, people's affective links to candidates and issues (Jeffres, 1997), and therefore to their political behavior, thus triggering participation, which is a central tenet of democracy. In the process, as part of the democratic ideal, consensus can emerge and national purpose can be pursued with unity. Much of the hype surrounding the Internet's democratic promise and potential can be traced back to the strong libertarian culture that has prevailed in America since the advent of new communications technologies and the Internet.

A radical example of this libertarian perspective is provided by cyber guru John Perry Barlow (1996), author and proponent of the 'Declaration of the Independence of Cyberspace' in which he confidently asserts:

> *Governments of the Industrial World, you weary giants of flesh and steel, I come from Cyberspace, the new Home of Mind. On behalf of the future, I ask you of the past to leave us alone. You are not welcome*

among us. You have no sovereignty where we gather. We have no elected government, nor are we likely to have one, so I address you with no greater authority than that with which liberty itself always speaks. I declare the global social space we are building to be naturally independent of the tyrannies you seek to impose on us. You have no moral right to rule us, nor do you possess any methods of enforcement we have true reason to fear ... (www.eff.org/~barlow/Declaration-Final.html, 10 Sep 2003).

With one stroke of the magic wand, cyber utopians like Barlow attempt to banish all government authority and declare the independence of cyberspace. Even more rational attempts to examine the impact of the Internet on government and politics manifest the same fantasies of a free and independent cyber space that will in time spread to the real world. These perspectives share a technologically deterministic vision and clearly underestimate the scope of political authority and power that continue to design, control and regulate much of cyberspace.

Several serious and critical studies have been undertaken in the past in order to delve into the correlation between the Internet and democratization (Kedzie, 1997; Norris, 2001; Hill and Hugues, 1999) and these studies have established some correlation between network connectivity and political freedom. However they do not conclusively determine causality and differ considerably on the extent of the impact of the Internet. In addition, Norris' (2001) study suggests that political change is a determinant of Internet diffusion and not vice-versa.

Robbles (2001) summarizes these four main characteristics of the Internet as its non-hierarchical architecture, its interactive nature and functionality, its global dimension as well as the near impossibility of controlling and regulating the medium. To what extent can these technical characteristics bring about greater democratization? How do these characteristics of the Internet play out in different national and political contexts?

THE NON-HIERARCHICAL ARCHITECTURE OF THE INTERNET

First, let us discuss the non-hierarchical architecture of the Internet. It is argued that the real transforming effect of the Internet is its capability to break down information hierarchy, which was one of the major obstacles to global information sharing witnessed in the development of earlier forms of media such as the print and broadcast media. It is generally argued that the unequal hierarchy of information dissemination that was prevalent with other forms of media and communication has been overcome by the open-ended and decentralized structure of the Internet.

Although, it is true that the Internet offers a more multidirectional flow of information than other media, it would be naïve to think that this technical feature actually allows for the breaking down of information hierarchies and monopolies. Transnational media corporations continue to dominate global information flows and have far greater resources and legitimacy than individuals or smaller groups and organizations when it comes to providing information and content. Moreover, and specifically in the Asian context, the state continues to maintain strict control over the media and information channels through regulation and ownership.

The Internet has in many ways dramatically enhanced information access and dissemination and provides a greater opportunity for people to access diverse forms of content as well as become providers of content themselves. Yet, provision of information and political content continues to be dominated by the very same players who have historically controlled global information flows, with but a few exceptions perhaps. Indeed, citizens' groups and civil society organizations as well as politically active individuals have seized on the potential of the Internet to disseminate information on a global scale to further their own political views and agenda. However, most often these agencies and individuals possess neither the news and information gathering capacity nor the legitimacy enjoyed by major national and international news and wire services to attract sufficient attention to their views.

The Internet's architecture alone is insufficient to break down the stranglehold of both the State and private corporations on information flows. Proponents of teledemocracy and cyber libertarians too often forget that numerous critical factors help to ensure the perpetuation of information hierarchies ranging from regulation and censorship and information filters to more direct and oppressive forms of censure and political punishment. Again, it is important to consider the fact that while in other areas of content distribution such as entertainment, the Internet has indeed brought about radical change through unrestricted global flows of content and information, when it comes to political information and news, restrictions always apply!

Politics continues to be confined to national issues and dynamics and until individuals, political parties and civil society at large actively participate in public debate and discussion, the Internet's non-hierarchical architecture is going to play a limited role in changing the political landscape.

THE INTERACTIVITY FACTOR

Let us now turn to another key characteristic of the Internet that is generally described as its interactivity. With the mass media, information flowed generally from a point or center to a mass audience with very limited channels of feedback and response for the recipients of information. Yes, there are the letters to the editor column for the newspaper and the call-ins for broadcasting, yet these feedback channels were extremely restricted by time, space and other constraints. It is argued that, with the Internet, users can shift from recipient to information provider with instant feedback opportunities. Moreover, the Internet offers any individual with the basic technological access and limited user skills the opportunity to become originators of information through the creation of individual or group websites as well as through their participation in chat rooms, discussion forums and other interactive sessions.

In this area, undoubtedly the Internet provides a new platform for multidirectional communication and information dissemination. The email has certainly transformed the ability of individuals to communicate instantaneously with individuals and groups across the world. Unlike other forms of mass media, the Internet provides greater possibilities of interaction and feedback. Whether it is through direct feedback on specific issues and topics covered by websites or through posting of individual opinions or even through real time live chats and bulletin board postings, the Internet has radically enhanced the individual's capacity to respond to and react to information available on the Internet and other sources.

However, one must consider the forces that trigger interactive usage of any medium. In the case of media such as broadcasting, which operates on the flow model or principle, the audience does not have to actively and systematically participate in content search and selection. But the Internet requires a high level of user participation and activity and this requires significant involvement on the part of users as well as greater levels of user motivation, activity and selectivity. It is more than evident then that if the user motivation is high then the Internet does provide a powerful tool for interactive communication and information dissemination.

This being said, it is also important to consider that user motivation is not sufficient in itself to trigger the active and political use of interactive technologies such as the Internet. A conducive political environment, which encourages political debate and participation and a state, which does not indulge in political censure and oppression, is also essential in promoting the use of the Internet for political debate and participation.

The key question here is what constitutes user motivation? Or does a specific national context and system encourage or discourage active involvement of citizens in the political process? I will argue that in undemocratic societies, the avenues for effective uses of interactive media technology generally are restricted through a variety of means, thereby neutralizing and limiting political motivation and consequently curtailing the full and effective use of interactive technologies like the Internet. In other words, even the most interactive technology does not have any political value if the political motivation of the user(s) is absent or limited and if the political environment restricts the usage of such a technology.

This is perhaps the dynamic that has stifled even the most ardent cries for democracy by citizens in most authoritarian and undemocratic regimes. When political motivation is high, regulations as well as overt and covert political pressures can still stifle political debate, dissent and participation. Furthermore, political motivation itself can be influenced through a process of 'de-politicization' that gradually creates a fearful and apathetic citizenry (Bedlington, 1978). Over time and under continued de-politicization, citizens can also lose all political motivation and this then dramatically reduces people's interest in political participation. The dismal voter turnout in elections in many nations around the world testifies to the increasingly widespread disenchantment of citizens vis-à-vis politics.

Every state exercises ideological and repressive measures to establish and cultivate the belief in its legitimacy (Weber, 1968, Althusser, 1994) in accordance with its right to govern (Heywood, 1999). In every state, the ruling power exercises a considerable amount of power on its citizens to ensure, amongst others, that social and political stability are maintained. According to Heywood (1999), this power is exercised at three levels:

(i)   The ability to manufacture or influence decisions,

(ii) The ability to set agenda and prevent decisions from being made,

(iii) The ability to manipulate what people think and want.

Such uses of political power and manipulation can have grave consequences on the ability of individuals and groups to challenge the hegemony of the state. The power of the state is further strengthened when it controls or restricts the use of information and communication technologies by citizens as this deprives them of critical means to participate in public debate, by voicing their opinions and providing critical inputs in the decision-making process. Thus those in most need of the media and the Internet remain the most deprived and this constitutes perhaps a significant challenge to the global spread of democracy.

The mere existence of interactive features of the Internet has little or no relevance for democratization, unless other necessary and critical conditions are in place. Here again, most studies have committed the fallacy of proclaiming the Internet's glorious democratic potential merely on some purely technical characteristic of the medium while omitting the socio-political conditions that drive the uses of such technologies in specific ways and contexts.

THE INTERNET'S GLOBAL DIMENSION

Yet another key feature of the Internet, namely its global dimension, has also been argued to constitute a powerful facet of the Internet's potential to enhance democratic practices. Again, unlike its predecessors, the Internet is a fundamentally global medium unlimited by spatial or geopolitical boundaries.

It is argued that, by opening nations to international and global information flows, the Internet provides citizens all over the world with a rich variety and diversity of information that can enhance both their understanding and the quality of their political participation. Perhaps the key contribution of this global dimension of the Internet to processes of democratization lies in its ability to overcome information filtering and control at the local and national levels.

In many Asian countries, where the media continue to be strictly controlled by the state, the advent of the Internet has opened out new political spaces and provides citizens with alternative views and critical information that were not available to them before. The advent of the Internet in China is thus argued to have contributed significantly to the democratic process in China and, interestingly, some studies have even argued that the Internet has radically changed the government's approach to information control. Indeed, Chinese political authorities are asking the state controlled media to be more accountable as a response to the growing popularity of the Internet in the country. They are strengthening their own media channels so as to avoid losing credibility in the presence of alternative sources of news and information (Ho, Kluver and Yang, 2003). The faith in the impact of global information flows through the Internet and its political impact has also been witnessed in some accounts of the fall of communism in Eastern Europe where the Soviet Union and other regimes' inability to control the flow of electronic information from outside is regarded is being one of the key reasons for its ultimate demise (Kalathil and Boas, 2003).

While this global dimension of the Internet and other electronic media can indeed contribute to the democratization process, it has to be contextualized and examined within specific national contexts. To begin with, while the Internet does enable global flows of information that offer vast amounts of political information to citizens across the world, the relevance of this information to local contexts and to the local political landscape is not always assured. Secondly, the diffusion of the Internet is even today very limited in most Asian countries and this continues to limit the diversity of political information available within Asia, thus maintaining and perpetuating the hegemony of the state, which continues to monitor, control and even produce much of the information that is available. This basic issue of access will be taken up in more detail later in this paper, but we will limit ourselves in highlighting the fact that access constitutes a key limitation in terms of the impact of global information flows on Asian politics and its efforts at democratization.

Even where citizens have access to foreign news and political information via the Internet, especially information and coverage that is critical of a particular nation's political system, it has been seen time and again that a given state can and does intervene in limiting such coverage through several coercive means, ranging from banning of foreign publications, monitoring citizens' access to specific websites as well as through active counter propaganda. Time and again, the recently retired Malaysian Prime Minister Mahathir Mohamed condemned international news and media coverage of Malaysia, accusing foreign news agencies and media institutions of leading a campaign to undermine the nation's image and credibility. China has also repeatedly censored and banned foreign media that is critical of its political system and authority. It continues to closely monitor the Internet and has not hesitated to use its political and economic power to punish its critics.

Thus the inherently global structure of the Internet has not eroded the power and authority of nation states to act against media coverage that is critical of any political establishment and its practices. In theory, anyone can access and post political information and news of any kind on the Internet. However, here again the real political world continues to influence political information and activity in cyberspace through a variety of coercive instruments that are at the disposal of the state machinery.

Finally, even the wholesale availability in Asia of a diverse range of networks and channels of political information that encourage criticism and dissent are not sufficient in themselves to trigger off greater political debate and participation. Information, although a key facilitator of democracy, is never enough in itself to establish democracy. The sheer availability of information or the mere existence of channels of information provision and access cannot in themselves guarantee political involvement and participation. The fundamental inequity of political power does not rest on inequity of information alone.

THE IMPOSSIBILITY OF REGULATING THE INTERNET?

The Internet is also regarded as a powerful democratic tool because of the professed impossibility of regulating the medium. Cyber libertarians believe that this feature of the Internet makes attempts at censorship and control a difficult, if not an impossible task. Robbles (2001) argued that even a repressive government, which opens its doors partially to the Internet, couldn't contain the flood of information, which then has a very strong democratizing effect on the country. The Internet, he emphasized metaphorically, is like a snowball, which is rolling and getting bigger. It gives everyone a voice, which is why it will still be going while those who seek to regulate it will have departed.

Developments in the Asian Internet landscape clearly belie the idea that the Internet escapes all forms of regulation and control. One can undoubtedly concede that the Internet, given its open ended and unique architecture, makes any form of regulation a difficult prospect. However, time and again, governments across Asia have found the necessary means to put in place legal and regulatory mechanisms to stop the medium from straying into what they perceived to be impermissible excesses. National security and stability, the need to preserve moral and ethical standards as well as breaches of the law have constituted strong arguments in favour of these regulatory mechanisms.

Recent studies have clearly demonstrated that the Internet has become a powerful tool in the hands of oppressive regimes, which have extensively used the medium for surveillance and control (Agre and Rotenburg, 1997; Kalathil and Boas, 2003). Lawrence Lessig (1999) has also convincingly argued that governments (democratic and authoritarian alike) can most certainly regulate the Internet, both by controlling its underlying code and by shaping the legal environment in which it operates. In fact, IP addresses leave a clear trace that can be easily and extensively used for surveillance, monitoring and for identifying individuals and groups who frequent specific sites or post certain kinds of content. This makes the job of policing the Internet much easier than is usually projected in discourses on Internet regulation and censorship.

In extreme authoritarian regimes, the Internet is simply banned and kept out of bounds for its citizens, as is the case with Myanmar. In semi-authoritarian nations such as Singapore, for example, Internet censorship and regulation help to maintain strict control over information while preventing effective uses of the medium by opposition parties and alternative political groups (Rodan, 1997; Banerjee and Yeo, 2003). China has systematically controlled the Internet, banning sites, censoring materials as well as using regulatory and technological means to restrict the political usage of the Internet. In his examination of the legislative, techno-logical and administrative strategies imposed by China's government, Qiu (1999/2000:23) contends that "China's Internet has taken a route of development deviating from its anticipated mission of democratization".

Singapore presents itself as a fascinating and essential case study of the ways in which a state can effectively regulate the Internet. In Singapore, there exists one of the most comprehensive strategies for development of IT anywhere in the world, supported by huge state-led infrastructure investments. It is evident that Singapore's policy makers are committed to the trans-formation of the island economy into an information hub, trading in ideas rather than commodities. However, Singapore's political leaders have no intention of surrendering political control in the process (Rodan, 1997).

Theoretically, the Internet represents a technical challenge for Singapore's "control-minded officials." However, the Government has attempted to impose strict broadcasting censorship on the medium (Rodan, 1997). The Internet is defined as a broadcast medium in Singapore (Ang & Nadarajan, 1997). The Government has emphasized that off-line rules also apply to the online world. The Singapore Broadcasting Authority (SBA) – a statutory board under the Ministry of Information, Telecommunication and the Arts (MITA) – regulates the Internet with the aim to safeguard public morals, political stability and religious harmony.

Singapore's strategy on Internet control is characterized by an attempt to bring this medium under the same tight regimen as other electronic and non-electronic media. Penalties are applied at various levels of information provision and authorship, including Internet service provision or newsgroup hosting (Rodan, 1997). Singapore made international headlines in 1995 by becoming the first country to establish censorship rules for the Internet (Ang, 1999).

On 20 July 2001, regulations were passed pertaining to the registration of political websites. Content providers of political websites are not required to clear their contents with Singapore Broadcasting Authority before publication. Under the SBA's Class License, all content providers are responsible for the content of their websites. Content providers who engage in the propagation, promotion or discussion of political issues relating to Singapore on World Wide Web through the Internet are required to be registered with the SBA. The objective of registering political websites is to ensure that those who run sites engaging in the discussion of domestic politics are accountable and take responsibility for the content of their sites. Under the Parliamentary Elections Amendment Bill, election advertising was disallowed on the Internet. It would be an offence for anyone to publish election advertising anywhere without identifying the printer, publisher or the person for whom the advertising is being done. The publication of election opinion polls would also be disallowed. Offenders could be fined $1,000 and jailed for 12 months.

Subsequently on 17 October 2001, the rules on Internet campaigning were spelt out under the Parliamentary Elections Act, amended in August 2002 to allow political parties to advertise on the Internet. The new rules however also cover e-mail and SMS messages. Political parties, candidates and election agents who send out email and SMS messages containing election advertising during an election must indicate who is sending the messages and on whose behalf they are sent. These should not include a 'chain letter' appeal.

Under these new regulations, party political websites are not allowed to conduct election surveys, appeals for election funds, and facilities allowing visitors to the site to search for disallowed forms of election advertising. Importantly, political parties must appoint moderators for chatrooms and discussion forums during the election and keep logs of all messages. The moderator must use his "best efforts" to ensure messages conform with the law, and remove messages the Returning Officer deems to be against public interest, public order or national harmony, or which offend good taste or decency (Tan, 2001).

The Singaporean regulatory environment thus demonstrates the state's ability to control the media and this disproves the contention that the Internet is beyond control and regulation. Numerous examples from Asia and other parts of the world indicate that, far from relinquishing control over the Internet, governments are finding new and innovative means to extend their hegemony over communication networks.

Governments in Asia have also used other tactics to control the Internet when they felt threatened by political views aired by both local and foreign individuals and groups. In Malaysia, for example, for several years following the ousting of former deputy-prime minister Anwar Ibrahim, Malaysiakini was allowed to post content that was critical of the government. The Malaysian government had clearly indicated that it would not resort to Internet censorship, and thereby created a space for alternative news and political debate. However, suddenly, on 20 January 2003, the Malaysian police raided Malaysiakini's offices, removed all the computers and servers and took them away for inspection and monitoring. The Malaysian police justified its raid on the Malaysiakini office by stating that they were investigating a report lodged by the UMNO Youth Organization (the youth wing of the ruling political party) on a seditious letter published on the Malaysiakini website.

In India, an investigative website Tehelka.com created a nation wide uproar by exposing the corruption of high level defense ministry officials who were video taped accepting bribes in exchange for lucrative defense contracts. This website, which was once internationally acclaimed for its investigative vigour and style, was then subjected to a series of investigations and accusations by the government that resulted in it losing potential investors and having to lay off most of its employees and journalists. Moreover, its journalists were harassed, hounded and even arrested by the government. This example illustrates the fact that even in relatively open democracies such as India serious challenges to the state that undermine its credibility can be punished and resisted through the use of the state's powerful institutions and agencies.

Models of Democracy and the Role of the Media: The Asian Dynamics
It is generally agreed that democracy is impossible without a free press (Baker, 2002). This view is based on the argument that more information and easier access to it leads to a better and informed citizenry, which in turn should lead to a greater power of citizens through more frequent forms of consultation. Information is regarded as being an essential pre-condition for full political participation (Curran, 1990).

The historical march towards democracy, however, reveals stark differences in different forms and practices of democracy around the world. Barber (2000/2001:3) argues that: "There is no such thing as democracy.

There are only a variety of forms of governments, which have a variety of characteristics that can be labeled under different groupings that define (not without controversy) distinctive forms of democracy". In this respect Young notes that:

> *Indeed, most societies have some democratic practices. Democracy is not an all-or-nothing affair, but a matter of degree: societies can vary in both the extent and the intensity of their commitment to democratic practice. Some or many institutions may be democratically organized, and in any such nominally democratic institution the depth of its democratic practice can vary"* (Young, 2000:5)

The existence of a variety of democratic forms and practices across the world undermine simplistic attempts to map the impact of the Internet on democracy in general or on a global scale. Barber (2000/2001) contends that asking whether the Internet has any impact on democracy is essentially meaningless. Research on this question must be contextualized to specific forms and practices of democracy in specific countries. Each model of democracy places a different emphasis on the role of information and the media to attain its objectives. Baker (2002) states that an assessment of the role of information and the media on any democracy first requires a theory of democracy.

Baker (2002) provides an extensive discussion on different models of democracies and political processes and the emphasis each of them places on the media and information. He examines the role of the media in elitist democracies as well as participatory models of democracy and contends that there are very clear differences in the role and emphasis placed on the media in different democratic and political systems.

An examination of democratic systems in Asia also indicates the different role and use of the media in various national contexts. It is impossible in a paper of this nature to characterize all the Asian democracies into specific models and to assess the respective role of media and information in each of these systems. I will therefore underline some key characteristics of Asian models of democracy and some salient features of their respective media systems.

Indeed, democracy in the contemporary sense of the term and understood in the context of nation states as a political unit, is a relatively new phenomenon in much of Asia given its colonial past. Many Asian nations, with the exception of countries such as China and Thailand, which never underwent Western colonial rule, began their march towards democracy after attaining their independence from their colonial masters. Thus began a new chapter in the political lives of these nations, which had to face the challenging task of creating modern nation-states and establish democratic regimes. The Asian political landscape is marked by a wide variety of models and systems ranging from authoritarian states to relatively developed democratic political systems.

The first critical obstacle in this new political landscape was the construction of a national identity. For most post-colonial nations, the task of nation building was strewn with difficulties and hardships. The objective in most cases was not only the constitution of a symbolic collective identity, that could reconcile the profound diversity that characterized these societies but also the very production and construction of a nation. Chua and Kuo aptly summarize this cultural dilemma and challenge in the Singaporean context:

> *These structural changes are all the more radical and their effects more impressive when one considers that Singapore as an independent nation-state was first and foremost a political reality foisted on a population under conditions beyond their control. Once this was a fait accompli, a 'nation' had to be constructed.* Chua and Kuo (1995:69)

The task of creating a national identity from a diversity of cultural, religious, ethnic and other constituents necessitated cautious planning and a wide array of programmes which temporarily curbed civil and political liberties in many Asian nations. Public debate was often restricted so as to avoid ethnic and religious conflict and the need to respect the diverse sensitivities that characterized the distinct communities also played a significant role in limiting the practice of democracy. Racial riots in Malaysia, Singapore, India, Indonesia and several other nations demonstrated the underlying tensions within fledgling Asian nations and these conflicts further heightened state vigilance and control, thus impeding the march of democracy.

Another related factor, which has affected processes of democratization in Asia, was the onerous task of national development. Most of these nations were faced with strong challenges ranging from underdevelopment and poverty, lack of social infrastructure, the task of reconciling imported institutions with indigenous traditions and problems of injustice and inequality. The state thus became omnipresent and omnipotent, centralizing all the executive, legislative and judicial powers in its fold. The lack of national commercial enterprises and the private sector contributed to this concentration of power in the hands of the state. Every aspect and problem of development had to be tackled by the state, which moreover was plagued by a severe shortage of human and material resources. The powerful Asian state was thus born and paved the way for various forms of abuse of power and political excess that have frustrated democratization efforts.

Asian democracies now stand at a critical crossroad. Most of them continue to be essentially 'plebiscite' democracies with the necessary institutional accoutrements including elections, parliamentary or presidential forms of government, as well as judicial, legislative and executive institutions. Young's satirical caricature of plebiscite democracy highlights one of the central weaknesses of most democracies in the world: "Even the supposedly most democratic societies in the world most of the time are largely 'plebiscite' democracies: candidates take vague stands on a few issues; citizens endorse one or another, and then have little relation to the policy process until the next election" Young (2000:5).

In Asia, many nations are still plagued by single party rule with no real opposition and continued perpetuation of injustice and inequality. Asian nations provide us with a wide range of democratic model and practices. Although it is difficult to characterize these diverse nations into specific models of democracy and, for purposes of general overview, we can borrow Gunaratne's (2000:9) model, which classifies Asian nations based on their religious and political characteristics as well as their degree of media freedom:

- Communist: Laos (Buddhist), China (Buddhist-Confucian), North Korea (Buddhist-Confucian), and Vietnam (Buddhist).

- Authoritarian (traditional monarchy, non-party presidential and military): Bhutan (Buddhist), Maldives (Islamic), Brunei Darussalam (Islamic), Myanmar (Buddhist), and post-coup Pakistan (Islamic).

- Dominant Party: Cambodia (Buddhist), Malaysia (Islamic), and Singapore (Buddhist-Confucian).

- Type II Parliamentary/Presidential Democracies with a Relatively Free Media System: Mongolia (Buddhist), India (Hindu), Post-Suharto Indonesia (Islamic), Sri Lanka (Buddhist), Bangladesh (Islamic), and Nepal (Hindu).

- Type I Parliamentary/Presidential Democracies with a Large Degree of Media Freedom: Thailand (Buddhist), Philippines (Christian), South Korea (Buddhist-Confucian/Christian), Taiwan (Buddhist-Confucian), and Japan (Buddhist-Shinto).

It can be argued that due to very different historical experiences and developments, most Asian nations have hybrid models of democracy, which are difficult to categorize according to the same models used in Western democratic theory. One can generally argue that nations such as India, the Philippines, Japan, Thailand, South Korea and Sri Lanka come closest to the participatory or deliberative models of democracy. Other nations such as Malaysia and Singapore practice an elitist model of democracy where it is believed that a country can be governed sensibly only by a vanguard leadership of elites or skilled experts. These countries implicitly believe that democracy is necessary because it is a better system than the alternatives and also because, in the modern world democracy is considered to be the only legitimate form of governance. Then there are yet other nations that continue to adhere to a communist worldview and have communist political systems. China, Cambodia, Laos and Vietnam among others have long histories as communist nations and only now are we witnessing slow and gradual transition towards some form of democracy in these countries.

Following from our earlier discussion, it can be then argued that these various forms of governance deploy very different media systems and assign various roles and functions to the media and information in the political process. Although generally the media in Asia, particularly broadcasting, have been subservient to the state, the last decade or so has seen radical transformations of the Asian media landscape. Deregulation and liberalization have created competitive and commercial media systems and the state's tight grip over the media seems to be somewhat eroded by these changes.

In the more complex and deliberative democracies, the media play a rich and diverse role providing a vibrant public sphere for contending political views and positions. For example, in India, Thailand, the Philippines, Japan and South Korea, the media are instrumental in promoting and protecting democracy. The media serve to provide the citizens with a diverse range of political views and opinions and allow them to express their views through active participation in public debate and discussion.

However, in the undemocratic and communist countries, the media continue to be tightly controlled by the state and - while there have been some changes in these media systems in China, Vietnam, Cambodia and others - the media certainly continue to be an instrument of government propaganda. In elitist democracies such as Malaysia and Singapore the role of the media is complex and - while there is an increasing and progressive trend towards privatization and commercialization - the state continues to maintain a tight grip over the media. The state wields its power over the media not only through a strict regulatory regime but also it continues to own media interests through its investment arms and government-linked companies.

What role can the Internet play in such a diverse range of political systems and regimes? Experiences of Internet use in more open and democratic societies tend to demonstrate quite a rich and diverse culture of political uses of the Internet. The Internet is being actively used by political parties, civil society and activist groups and the citizenry at large. Political discussion groups, websites providing alternative political views, chat-rooms where political issues are openly discussed and debated are beginning to proliferate in most of these countries. The Internet is essentially providing a flexible and interactive platform for political debate and participation in many of these nations. The Internet can be seen in nations such as India, Sri Lanka, Thailand, Japan and South Korea as enhancing the avenues for access and dissemination of political information. The Internet is offering to the citizens what the mass media, due to their inherent technical limitations and centralized architecture, could not provide.

However, it is important to note that democratic practices and active citizen involvement in political debate and participation existed before the advent of the Internet in many of these nations. The Internet is providing individuals and groups with new capabilities and modes of political participation through enhanced access to information. It is also offering multi-directional participatory platforms to citizens for greater consultation, feedback and dialogue.

In communist and elitist nations in Asia, the role of the Internet differs in many ways to the uses in more open and democratic societies. Even within communist nations there are significant differences and the role and use of the Internet in China is fundamentally different from experiences in other nations such as Cambodia and Vietnam. It is not my intention here to present a detailed description of the specific potential and uses of the Internet in different Asian nations. What I am essentially pointing out is the critical necessity to consider different models and forms of democracy and the specific ways in which the Internet is playing a role in enhancing public debate and political participation. This must constitute a key dimension of any attempt to map the democratic use and potential of the Internet.

POLITICAL PARTICIPATION AND THE ROLE OF THE INTERNET

An overview of the literature on the political impact of the Internet reveals that the central thesis in much of the growing body of literature in this suggests that the key impact of the Internet on democracy follows from its ability to enhance political debate, mobilization and participation. The Internet is said to be providing radically new forms of information access and dissemination that are critical for the active participation of citizens in the political arena. As political participation, especially in participatory theories of democracy, is a measure of democratic politics, the Internet thus becomes a major tool for democratization.

Here again, I will highlight certain theoretical and methodological weaknesses of a significant body of literature on the Internet's democratic potential. To begin with, there are very different forms of political participation. Milbrath (1965) identifies several forms of political participation, which can be categorized generally as: spectatorial, transitional and gladiatorial. Each of these forms of political participation reflects different levels of citizen engagement in politics. Most citizens are spectatorial participants in the political process as they are content to perform their basic duties as citizens, vote, read about and discuss politics occasionally. The transitional forms of political participation require more engagement and involvement on the part of citizens. In this category of participants we find people who are more engaged, more likely to participate actively in political debate, public demonstrations and actively promote their view of political candidates and issues. Finally, there are the gladiatorial participants, consisting of fully engaged political individuals who not only indulge in all the activities of the other two categories of political participation but also are directly involved in politics, are members of political parties or even candidates and generally tend to be political activists. It must be noted however that these categories are not cast in stone and citizens often move from one form of political participation to another depending on the issues at stake, their own personal interest and other critical factors.

In assessing the political impact of the Internet, it is thus important to examine the differentiated uses of the Internet in various forms of political participation. It can be argued that, for example, a political activist is much more likely to fully utilize the participatory potential offered by the Internet than a spectatorial participant. We can also agree that for a strictly spectatorial form of political participation the Internet is not really necessary or even relevant.

Another dimension that requires close attention is the issue of political motivation. Political participation is itself driven by political motivation. When political motivation is high and citizens show high levels of commitment and engagement to political decisions and processes, then the Internet can become a powerful tool with positive feedback and externalities. The opposite also holds true: that is, when political motivation is low and citizens' engagement in politics is weak, then the capabilities offered by the Internet simply become irrelevant. As such, any discussion on the political or democratic role and impact of the Internet must pay attention to the specific issues at hand and the levels and factors of political motivation.

It needs to be further added that political motivation and the ensuing political participation themselves can be conditioned by a wide variety of factors. An examination of the Asian political landscape clearly reveals the fact that in some nations, the state strives to minimize and restrict political participation. This is achieved sometimes through the rights guaranteed by the constitution including freedom of speech and expression and the right to assembly and peaceful demonstration and sometimes through political censure and various regulatory mechanisms. In authoritarian states, even overt and covert political punishment is used to minimize political participation, especially when citizens manifest their dissent and publicly demonstrate their dissatisfaction with political regimes and their policies.

My contention is that all these different factors and context-related variables need to be taken into consideration in any examination of the role and impact of the Internet on political change and democratization. While the media and the Internet provide certain possibilities for enhancing political participation, these possibilities are regulated by the forces and constraints of each political system. It is naïve however, to assume that the mere presence of tools for enhanced political participation can turn all citizens of a nation into political activists and gladiatorial participants.

REFERENCES

Agre, Philip E., and Marc Rotenberg, eds. (1997). *Technology and Privacy: The New Landscape*. Cambridge: MIT Press.

Althusser, L . (1994). *The Future Lasts Forever: A Memoir*. New York: Doubleday/ New York Press.

Ang, P.H. (1999). "Information Highways – Policy and Regulation: The Singapore Experience." In V. Iyer (Ed.), *Media regulations for new times* (pp. 97-114). Asian Media Information and Communication Centre, Singapore.

Banerjee, I. (2003). *Rhetoric and Reality: The Internet Challenge for Democracy in Asia*. Singapore: Eastern Universities Press.

Baker, C. E. (2002). *Media, Markets and Democracy*. New York: Cambridge University Press.

Barber, B. R. (2000/2001) "Which Technology For Which Democracy? Which Democracy For Which Technology?", International Journal of Communication Law and Policy, Issue 6, Winter 2000/2001.

Barlow, J. P. (1996). A Cyberspace Independence Declaration. www.eff.org/ Publications/John_Perry_Barlow/barlow_0296.declaration

Bedlington, S. (1978). *Malaysia and Singapore: The building of new states*. Ithaca: Cornell University Press.

Chua,B.H., and Kuo, E.C.Y. (1995) "The making of a new nation", in Beng Huat, C., *Communitarian Ideology and Democracy in Singapore*, London: Routledge.

Curran, J. (1990) "The New Revisionism in Mass Communication Research: A Reappraisal", *European Journal of Communication* 5: 130-64.

Dahlberg, L. (2001). "Computer-Mediated Communication and The Public Sphere: A Critical Analysis", *Journal of Computer Mediated Communication*. Vol 7 No.1.

Dutton, William H. (1992) "Political Science Research on Teledemocracy". In: *Social Science Computer Review*, 10(4), Winter, pp. 505-522.

Gunaratne, S.A. (2000) "Overview" in Gunaratne, S.A. (ed.) *Handbook of the Media in Asia*, New Delhi: Sage.

Heywood, A. (1999), *Political Theory: An Introduction*, (2nd ed.), USA: St. Martin's Press, Inc.

Hill, Kevin A., and John E. Hughes. (1998). *Cyberpolitics: Citizen Activism in the Age of the Internet*. Lanham, MD: Rowman and Littlefield.

Ho, K.C., Kluver, R., and Yang, C. C. (Eds.). (2003). *Asia Encounters the Internet*. London: Routledge.

Jeffres, L.W. (1997), *Mass Media Effects*, 2nd Ed, USA: Waveland Press, Inc.

Kalathil, S and Boas, C.T. (2003). *Open Networks, Closed Regimes*. Washington D.C.: Carnegie Endowment for International Peace.

Kedzie, Christopher. (1997). 'The Third Waves', in *Kahin and Neeson (eds) 1997*.

Kedzie, Christopher R. (1997) "A Brave New World or a New World Order?" in *Culture of the Internet*, Sara Kiesler (ed.), Mahwah, NJ: Lawrence Erlbaum Associates, Inc.

Lessig, Lawrence. (1999). *Code and Other Laws of Cyberspace*. New York: Basic Books.

Masuda Y. (1981). *The Information Society as Post-Industrial Society*. Bethesda, MD.: World Future Society.

Mosco, V. (1989), "The pay-per Society." in *Computers and Communication in the Information Age*, NJ, USA: Ablex Publishing Corporation.

Milbrath, L. (1965). *Political Participation*. Chicago: Rand McNally.

Naisbett, J. (1982). *Megatrends*. New York: Warner Books, Inc.

Norris, Pippa. (2001). *Digital Divide: Civic Engagement, Information Poverty, and the Internet Worldwide*. Cambridge: Cambridge University Press.

Robbles, A.C. (2001). "The Internet and Democracy." in *Panorama* 3/2001. Germany:

Rodan, G. (1997). "The Internet And Political Control In Singapore." In *Political Science Quarterly 113, (Spring 1998)*, 63-89.

Tan T.H. (2001). "Rules on E-Campaigning Spelt Out." *The Straits Times*, 18 October

Toffler, A. (1981). *The Third Wave*, New York: William Morrow.

Weber , M. (1968). *Economy and Society*, ed. by G. Roth and C. Wittich. New York: Bedminster Press.

Young, I.M. (2000). *Inclusion and Democracy*. New York: Oxford University Press.

CHAPTER 3

Images of E-Government
Experiences from the Digital North Denmark

ARNE REMMEN

INTRODUCTION

As part of the Digital North Denmark participatory research has been carried out in order to track changes within different areas like e-government and at the same time take part in discussions regarding new perspectives and further development in relation to digital administration.

This article will give an overview of the general use of information and communication technologies (ICT) in Denmark as a background for looking more into depth regarding the experiences with e-government in the Digital North Denmark. The projects related to e-government will be examined related to objectives and means, as well as incentives and barriers. The municipalities have taken quite different approaches to e-government that is clear from both the different understandings and implementation strategies. The major differences between the municipalities regarding preconditions, understandings and strategies are evident in the different images of e-government among the municipalities in North Denmark.

USE OF INFORMATION AND COMMUNICATION TECHNOLOGY IN DENMARK

Several investigations have been made that highlight the use of ICT in public administration, and to what extent the Danish population have access to and are using the Internet.

The readiness for the "networked world" is measured every year several on the basis of indicators in The Global Information Technology Report (Dutta, *et al.*, 2003). Different Danish governments' preparations to enable the population to take advantage of ICT are paying off in terms of high level of Networked Readiness, and in Denmark's' overall ranking as number eight in the world. The indicators are within three main areas: the environment index 11 (market, regulation and infrastructure), the readiness index 11 (availability, costs, etc.) and the usage index 6 (number and use of ICT). (Dutta, *et al.*, 2003:210).

In a recent report "Information Society Denmark" from the Danish Ministry of Science, Technology and Innovation, a status is made regarding the use of ICT products in Denmark Over 80% of the population has a PC, and even more have a mobile telephone. Nearly 80% have access to the Internet from home or from the workplace, and there is no major gender difference. In general, the access to the Internet is around 80-85% for all ages, but with two major exceptions: 94% of young people between 16 to 19 years have access; and only 44% of people older than 60 have access. (Ministry of Science and Statistics Denmark, 2003)

Over 55% of the population use the Internet to receive and send e-mails, and around 50% to find information on services and goods. The third most popular purpose of using the Internet is to be in contact with public authorities, which around 40% are on a regular basis. Internet banking/financial service is used by 35% while more than 25% read or download online news, and nearly the same counts for e-commerce. The Icelandic population uses the Internet significantly more in all areas, except for e-commerce. The patterns of use are to some extent rather similar in Denmark, Sweden and Finland. However, the Internet is used by less than 5% of the Danes for educational purposes, while in Finland nearly 30% and in Iceland more than 40% use it for these purposes.

DIFFUSION OF ICT IN THE PUBLIC SECTOR

It has been the policy of changing Danish governments to support the diffusion of the Internet through the implementation of e-government. Public authorities should provide the serious content on the net. Today, 70% of the firms with

Internet access use it for communication with public authorities, and as mentioned four out ten citizens are doing the same. At the same time, the public authorities are developing new digital services to both companies and citizens that will increase the use of digital administration further.

The effects of digitalisation projects in state institutions, countries and municipalities have been analysed in a recent report. Especially the counties – but also a majority of state institutions and municipalities – have experienced positive benefits like adjustments of work procedures and new competence. However, when it comes to freeing up resources (another word for higher efficiency) more than 50% of state institutions and municipalities have only had few or no resource savings. (Statistics Denmark, 2002

Table 1: Effects of digitised projects (Statistics Denmark, 2002)

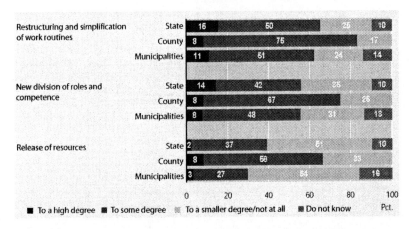

Note: The authorities were asked to which degree the digitised projects carried out over the past 2 years had changed the way tasks were handled in relation to how they were handled previously. Answers were given in relation to the areas included in the digitisation.

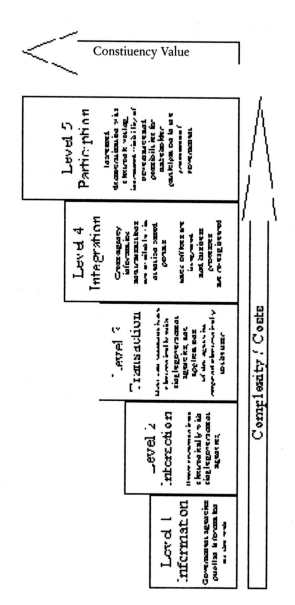

Figure 1: Maturity of e-government (adapted from Abramson and Means, 2001)

The overall impression is that especially the municipalities are on very different levels regarding ambitions and preconditions for implementation and use of e-government. Several municipalities have, only within the last three years, made a home page for dissemination of information, and begun digitalisation of internal work processes (like level 1 in the figure below).

Other municipalities, the counties and many state institutions have moved on to what can be called the 2nd generation of e-government focussing on public service, on-line communication with industry and citizens, and internal improvement of competence and organisational development (level 2 and 3 in figure 1). Some of the front-runners are now developing new digital services, and have much more focus on inter-organisational collaboration crossing borders and boundaries among public authorities.

In the report Benchmarking e-government: A Global Perspective (UN, 2002) the United Nations and American Society for Public Administration are using a similar model to figure 1 in order to measure and benchmark the progress of e-government in the UN member states. In the report five stages of e-government is set up as a method for quantifying the progress. The stages "are representative of the governments level of development based primarily on the content and deliverable services through official web-sites" (UN, 2002: 11).

The five stages are:

Emerging: An official government online presence is established.

Information is limited, basic and static.

Enhanced: Government sites increase.

Content and information is updated with greater regularity.

Interactive:Users can download forms, contact officials and make appointments and requests.

Transactional:Users can pay for services or conduct financial transactions online.

Seamless:Full integration of e-functions and services across administrative boundaries.

According to the UN report, not a single country in the world has reached the "seamless" stage, 17 countries are measured to be in the transactional stage and 55 countries are regarded to be in the interactive stage, including Denmark.

These stages and the levels in figure 1 are from an e-government perspective asking the questions: to what degree are information and services available? And to what extent are government and users of public services interacting on-line? In other words, the citizen and democracy perspective is underexposed, and the linkages and connections between these two perspectives need to be more highlighted.

DIGITAL NORTH DENMARK AND E-GOVERNMENT

The Digital North Denmark was created at the beginning of 2000 as an experiment with the network society. The main objectives have been:

- To create the future networked society
- To try out experiments aimed at tomorrow's IT society

The total budget was 90 million Euros, and funding has been provided for 90 development projects within different areas. Furthermore, a "lighthouse" secretariat was created in order to co-ordinate the projects. (For more information see www.DetDigitaleNordjylland.dk and the article by Nanna Skovrup).

Within the area of e-government several projects were funded:

- Digital Democracy in Rural Areas
- Digital Service for the Citizens of North Denmark
- Openness in Digital Administration and the Press as a Mediator
- The ABDD Portal
- The Active Map of Aalborg
- The Digital County Administration
- The Digital Democracy

- The Open Digital Administration

- The [Inter] Active Citizen

- Towards the Digital Town Hall

- Your Open Municipality

- Digital Administration for the Future

Nearly all the projects focus on e-government, and two to three projects pay special attention to e-democracy.

Furthermore, six interdisciplinary research projects were funded at Aalborg University involving five different departments within the following areas:

- E-democracy

- E-government

- ICT and infrastructure

- E-learning

- ICT in the health sector

- Business development and the ICT sector

The research related to e-government has been carried out in three inter-related steps. First, an analysis was made of the objectives and means in the initial project descriptions of the above projects (Remmen and Larsen, 2002). Secondly, a PhD project was initiated and a researcher focused on the use of ICT in planning – making a detailed case study of two projects. Finally, an investigation was carried out based on twenty interviews conducted in the fall of 2003 with project leaders, ICT managers, managing directors of municipalities and the North Jutland County. The aim was to map out the experiences with e-government both in the seven municipalities actively involved in the above projects and in five municipalities that had not taken part in any projects within this area in the Digital North Denmark (Remmen, Larsen and Mosgaard, 2004). The following description and analysis is based on this material and on the results from a quantitative investigation of e-government from spring 2003 (PLS, 2003).

IMAGES OF E-GOVERNMENT – OBJECTIVES AND MEANS

Most of the e-government projects have rather broad *objectives* including both efficiency, development of public services for the users, and democratisation paying attention to the citizens. Based on impressions of the interviews, the most important features have been efficiency, public services and modernisation of the public administration.

In general, there is an "unspoken" objective regarding *modernisation* of the public administration is to be able to match changes in other parts of society. One of the municipalities talks about the "the law of necessity" in the sense that the municipalities need set a good example for local industry, by improving their services, and furthermore attract well-qualified employees. In other words, the municipalities have to be the driving force among the local stakeholders in order to take advantage of the ICT potentials.

In the project descriptions, the objectives are broadly outlined and in most project all three objectives: efficiency, services and democratisation are stressed (see the summary below). However, in the interviews focus was clearly on efficiency and public services, while democratisation mainly was on the agenda in the two projects with this special focus. In other words, in most of the projects the population is seen as users of public services rather than as citizens with legitimate interests in participation and influence.

Objectives	Efficiency	Public Service	Democracy
	Cost reductions	Better quality Easy access (24 hours) New services	Participation Interactive dialogue

Digitalisation of work processes, enhancement of competence, and organisational development have been such important cornerstones in the e-government projects that these means can be considered as indirect objectives – or in other words necessary, internal conditions for achieving the long-term objectives.

Technical change and implementation of the hardware had a dominant role in earlier projects within this area (Kofoed and Remmen, 1992). Today, most of the project leaders and the directors of municipalities know that technology only is 20% while organisational development constitutes 80% of the effort in implementation of e-government. However, at the same time it is underlined as a precondition that the technical solutions simply must work, and partly as a joke it was said in one of the interviews that the efforts more often turns out to be 80% - 80%. Furthermore, the interviews also give a clear impression that courses, development of competence, etc. are considered to be much more important by the organisations than before, and compared to ten years ago especially the young employees have much better ICT qualifications.

Means	Technical change	Competence	Organisational development
	Infrastructure Digitalisation	Qualifications Knowledge sharing	Internal and external collaboration Re-organising work processes

Both objectives and means have been adjusted during the implementation, which shows an experimental and flexible approach in the projects and openness for adjustments along with new experiences – in other words learning. This can also be seen as an indicator that implementation of e-government is not a routine task and that the municipalities lack the preconditions for making detailed planning of the projects.

BARRIERS TO E-GOVERNMENT

In the interviews several restrictions related to the lack of resources in the municipalities were emphasised. Furthermore, three barriers were highlighted:

a. Danish municipalities are occupied with routine tasks, and the capacity for innovation and change is too small,

b. Bureaucracy – too little attention on continuous improvements of work tasks and routines,

c. Mr. usual – no tradition for thorough changes of the organisation.

There was a tendency that especially the small municipalities stressed the lack of resources both regarding staff, competence, and financial resources as an explanation for falling behind with the implementation of e-government.

The big municipalities have in most cases been involved in several projects related to e-government, and they were especially stressing cultural barriers (as mentioned above). In other words, especially the front-runners in e-government are stressing the necessity to change the traditional image that public administration is dusty and bureaucratic.

Another barrier mentioned in several interviews is that the Danish government has planned to make a structural adjustment of the public sector resulting in fewer municipalities and counties as well as a new division of tasks in the public administration. Among the small municipalities this has created uncertainty about the future and it seems that most small municipalities are just waiting to see what will happen.

The specific context and conditions in the municipalities are crucial for whether a factor is being considered as a barrier or a means. Some of the factors mentioned in the interviews are considered in both ways. The commitment of the administrative top management is for example seen as a necessary condition for implementation of e-government, in cases with lack of commitment it is seen as an important barrier.

The employees and the users/citizens have the same double role as drivers and barriers. In some cases, the employees have been highly motivated, initiated the idea, developed it further and have taken actively part in the implementation of the project, while in other cases there have been resistance towards change among some employees. Also when it comes to the users of public services, some see e-government as an opportunity to have easy access to existing and new public services 24 hours a day, and possibly increase their influence on the local policy as citizens. However others may not have access or they may rather want contact to the public administration in person.

The Digital North Denmark has been important for overcoming most of the barriers. The external, financial support has been an incentive for especially the small municipalities to increase their e- government activities, but also for the major players it has given an opportunity to realise some of the more comprehensive visions, and it has created a kind of synergy and competition among the front-runners. Certainly e-government is higher up on the agenda in the municipalities in North Jutland than five years ago.

A survey made by PLS has also highlighted the barriers to e-government. The survey is showing a rather small difference in the tendencies among the municipalities in North Jutland compared to all Danish municipalities, but it is worth noticing that all municipalities in North Jutland have participated in the survey and not only the ones engaged in e-government projects. The answers regarding barriers are outlined in the table below.

Table 2: Barriers to implementation of e-government

		To a high degree	To some degree	To a smallller degree	Not at all	Do not know
Lack of central public control and counselling	NKA DK	0% 13%	30% 41%	48% 30%	4% 13%	17% 3%
Lack of resources in public organisations	NKA DK	26% 28%	65% 48%	9% 13%	0% 9%	0% 2%
The advantage of a transition to e-government is too small in comparison to costs	NKA DK	30% 26%	35% 46%	22% 15%	9% 9%	4% 5%
Lack of knowledge among the citizens of what e-government can offer	NKA DK	4% 31%	61% 52%	17% 15%	13% 1%	4% 1%
Citizen's resistance to use of e-government	NKA DK	0% 4%	39% 43%	26% 41%	30% 9%	4% 3%
Lack of interest in handing over/ restructuring tasks between public institutions	NKA DK	9% 15%	39% 56%	35% 18%	13% 8%	4% 3%

NKA: North Jutland Municipalities and County - DK: Denmark
(PLS, 2003, p.42)

One of the interesting findings were that on the national level and within 2/3 of the municipalities in North Jutland answered that the benefits from e-government were *to a high* or *to some degree* too small compared to the costs. This result is perhaps even more noticeable when it is taken into account that the people responsible for ICT in the municipalities answered the question.

Table 3: Barriers to e-government (Statistics Denmark, 2002, p. 87)

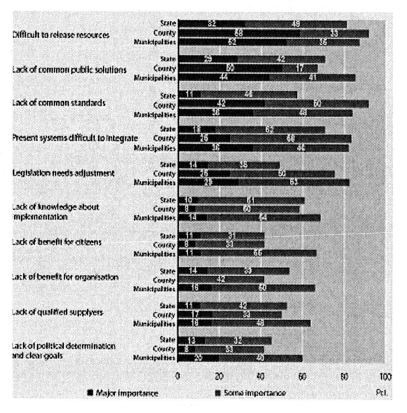

The national survey of the use of ICT in the public sector also examined the barriers to e-government (Statistics Denmark, 2002). The barriers towards e-government were considered to be higher than the general barriers towards ICT. Most authorities found it difficult to release resources to e-government and around 90% of all counties and municipalities found this barrier to have some or high importance with more than 50% seeing this as a major obstacle.

Around seven out of ten authorities lacked common public ICT solutions and infrastructure, and around the same number lacked common standards for exchange of data and did also find it difficult to integrate existing systems. These three barriers were especially seen as problems by municipalities and counties, but also 60 to 70% of the state institutions were stressing these areas as problems. 82% of the municipalities and 75% of the counties found that the existing laws and regulations needed adjustment, while this was "only" found necessary by 50% of the state institutions. Lack of knowledge about implementation, lack of benefits for the citizens, lack of qualified suppliers as well as lack of political commitment and clear targets were other examples of barriers mentioned in the survey (Statistics Denmark, 2002)

RESULTS FROM THE PROJECTS REGARDING E-GOVERNMENT

A frequent answer to the question about the results of the e-government projects in the Digital North Denmark is that it is too early to measure, and the project managers expect to have a much clearer picture of the results in 2004.

As mentioned, higher efficiency has been an important objective. The municipalities give a lot of specific examples on how e-government has saved time and money, because all internal and still more of the external communication has been digitised. All agendas and minutes are available on the Intranet as electronic records save time and space fewer copies are produced, and it saves stamps, etc. However, few of the municipalities are trying to keep a clear record of the higher efficiency.

Another result highlighted by the respondents is improved public services. The examples given are improved information to the citizens through home pages, easier access to the civil servants via e-mails, on-line forms that can be out, different kinds of transactions, etc.

A discussion which has taken place in many municipalities have been, to what extent should higher efficiency be used to improve working conditions for the employees, reduce man-power, and/or improve public services. There is not a single approach to this issue – the municipalities are different and unique regarding preconditions, culture, previous experiences with ICT, etc. Therefore, quite different implementation strategies have been successful in different settings. The politicians in Aalborg Municipality had openly demanded a reduction of employees by 5%, and it was considered beneficial for the projects that this was a clear condition from the beginning. In Frederikshavn municipality they believe that it would have been a major problem for the projects, if this had been a demand; because they couple of years earlier had made some reductions among the employees due to a digitalisation project.

Especially the front-runners in e-government stress the importance of the internal benefits in the organisation like having a comprehensive vision, readiness for change, adjustment of attitudes, a more dynamic culture, new ways of doing things, etc. Only the county and a few big municipalities stressed the importance of knowledge sharing in the organisations. One respondent highlighted that in the old, bureaucratic organisation a lot of time was used on moving information up and down, while now the employees themselves are taking responsibility for their work tasks and for finding the necessary information.

In the survey by PLS, questions have also been asked regarding the effects of e-government. The general picture was the same: a soft result like improved exchange of information was especially stressed; while only a little more than 20% of the respondents to some degree experienced financial and resource savings. An important part of the picture was that more than 20% answered "donot know". It indicates, in line with the interviews, that none of municipalities had clear routines or tools for measuring the results of the projects.

CONCLUSION

As a way of concluding this chapter we shall sum up the major conclusions related to e-government from the interviews with municipalities and the county in the Digital North Denmark, and discuss the different images of e-government in general.

Large variations
The municipalities are at different stages and on very different levels. The county and a few large municipalities are moving from being interactive to

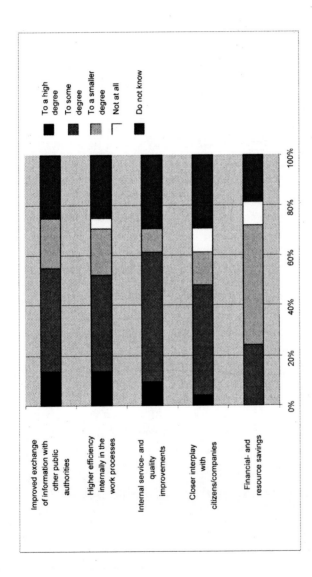

Table 4: The level of effects experienced in North Jutland (PLS, 2003, p.54)

transactional, and there is an increasing awareness among their project managers that boundaries need to be crossed. They are considered front-runners and have been engaged in several projects in the Digital North Denmark. At the same time, several small municipalities in North Jutland are lacking behind because of few financial resources, lack of employees with ICT qualifications, etc. They are moving from "emerging" to "enhanced", but are mainly waiting to see what is happening to the structural reform of the public administration.

Focus inside the public administration

The projects regarding e-government have had a focus within the each administrative unit, even in cases where the projects were initiated in collaboration with several municipalities and other stakeholders. However, all municipalities agreed that 1 September 2003 should be e-day. From then on electronic communication between authorities and between authorities and users should be permitted, and later they also committed themselves to implement digital signature.

Different images of the objectives

At least three different images of e-government were present in the objectives of the approved projects: efficiency, service and democracy. In the project descriptions all three objectives were mentioned, but with greatest focus on efficiency and public services. This was even more so in practise, except for one to two projects paying special attention to democracy.

Different images of means

Some of the means like digitalisation of information and work processes as well as organisational development were important that the means became the ends. For many of the municipalities this was a necessary first step in order to maintain such objectives as efficiency and new services.

80% technical change and 80% organisational development

Most of the project managers were conscious that e-government was 20% hardware and 80% organisational change. Compared to previously, competence and organisational development were much higher up on the agenda. However it is a precondition for the projects that the technical solutions are working, hence the reality has become 80% - 80%.

Different images of implementation strategies – not one best way
Some have made changes in an area of an administration, while others have had an integrated strategy for the whole municipality. Some have focused on detailed planning, while others just started. Some were relying on local "entrepreneurs" among the employees, while others had an overall strategy and a strong top-management commitment. Some strategies were better than others, however it was notable that different implementation strategies worked in different settings – there is not one best way to e-government.

Learning – ends and means change during the process
Ends and means were adjusted during the process, due to an experimental and flexible approach open to learning from new experiences. This in part indicates that such projects are not common in small municipalities that lack traditions for coping with uncertainty, constant change, etc.

Focus on possibilities – not on disadvantages
A common characteristic of the e-government projects was that the focus was only on advantages and possibilities for using ICT in public administration; none of the projects were really dealing with disadvantages and risks.

Network society - without networking
Digital North Denmark has experimented with the Network Society – the focus has been on diffusion rather than on innovation of high tech solutions. However, network collaboration regarding e-government has so far been limited. Recently, a platform has been created and the municipalities are more ready for network collaboration than before.

E-government is high on the agenda, but e-democracy and e-governance is not
The use of ICT in the public sector is now high on the agenda in the municipalities, but so far in most cases with an intra-organisational focus: *e-administration*. Especially the large municipalities and the county have also had an inter-organisational focus: *e-government* as a new way to deliver efficient, 24 hours public services. However, steps towards *e-governance* draw on a different image of what the public sector is and how it ought to work – it will have much more focus on transparency, democracy in decision-making and network interactions between citizens, governmental bodies, NGOs, etc.

REFERENCES

Danish Ministry of Science, Technology and Innovation, and Statistics Denmark, 2003: *Information Society Denmark, ICT Status 2003*

Denmark's Statistics, 2002: *Den offentlige sektors brug af it.* (The Use of IT in the Public Sector).

Dutta, Soumitra, *et al.*, (eds.) 2003: *The Global Information Technology Report 2002-2003. Readiness for the Networked World.* Oxford University Press.

www.DetDigitaleNordjylland.dk

Kofoed, Lise Busk and Arne Remmen, 1991: "Information Technology in Local Administration", in *Danish Experiments - Social Constructions of Technology.* The Committee in Technology and Society, The Danish Social Science Research Council.

Remmen, Arne and Torben Kjeldgaard Larsen, 2002: *Digital forvaltning og fysisk planlægning – set i forhold til den lærende region.* Work note, Department of Development and Planning, Aalborg University.

Remmen, Arne; Torben Kjeldgaard Larsen, and Mette Mosgaard, 2004: *Digital forvaltning i Nordjylland. – Forventninger, erfaringer og resultater*, Aalborg University.

PLS Rambøll Management, 2003: *Det digitale Nordjylland. Statusbillede af digital forvaltning i Nordjylland*, Rambøl Management.

UN, Division for Public Economics and Public Administration and American Society for Public Administration, 2002: *Benchmarking E-government: A Global Perspective. Assessing the Progress of the UN Member States.*

CHAPTER 4

E-Regulation in Asia
The Internet and a Freer Asia

PENG HWA ANG

One of the powers attributed to the new medium of the Internet is its supposed democratizing influence. It (the Internet) is supposed to transfer power from the government to the citizen. It is supposed to empower individuals at the expense of government. Perhaps the key trait is its supposed ability to bypass censorship.

In Asia, however, the 'Net seems not to have had such salutary effects. There are frequent reports of new Internet regulations that are censorial in one form or another. In fact, an oft-used bogeyman of regulation is to say that the regulating the Internet would be acting like the governments of two Asian countries—China and Singapore.

This paper argues that the Internet will indeed make Asia, including China and Singapore more free, although not at the pace or in the direction that free speech advocates and civil libertarians the world over might hope for.

CONVENTIONAL REASONS
Large historical force—free market capitalism has won

There are two main reasons implicitly or explicitly given for the Internet making the world freer—one based on economics and the other on technology. Both are deficient.

The first argument is that free market capitalism has won. No technology can be set apart from its context and in today's context free market capitalism has won. There is no other political system that poses as a serious alternative. Free market capitalism requires information to grease the economic cogs. Accountability is not through a central accounting body; instead it is transparency that is the means of accountability. Planning is not by a central planning body; it is the market that decides. Both transparency and market mechanisms require information to function properly. In short, unless a country wishes to cut itself off from the rest of the economic world, it has to encourage the flow of information if it wishes to base its economy on free market capitalism. The economic ideology of the times is on the side of the freer flow of information.

The force of this argument, however, is limited because it argues the case for freer economic but not political information. Such a division of information is artificial; one segment of life cannot be sealed off from another. Every segment impinges on another. And political information is the nub of what free speech is about. The free market argument falls short where it is most needed.

THE CENSORSHIP-BYPASSING TECHNOLOGY

The second line of argument is that it is difficult to censor the Internet. The usual reason given is that the Internet treats censorship as damage and bypasses it. A recent report by Reporters Sans Frontieres titled "Enemies of the Internet" sums up the argument thus:

> Moreover, web surfers can find ways round censorship: encoding, going through servers that offer anonymity when consulting banned sites or sending email, connecting via GSM telephones and cellphones, and so on (2001, www.rsf.fr/uk/home.html).

It then went on to list 20 countries that it considered the enemy of the Internet. But this begs the question: if governments cannot censor the Internet, how can there be enemies of the Internet? It is hopeless to be an enemy of an invincible foe. The answer is that the Internet can be censored, within limits. And indeed, the preceding paragraph in the report mentions some examples:

> On the pretext of protecting the public from "subversive ideas" or defending "national security and unity", some governments totally prevent their citizens from gaining access to the Internet. Others control a single ISP or even several, installing filters blocking access to web sites regarded as unsuitable and sometimes forcing users to officially register with the authorities. (*Ibid.*)

So where are the fallacies in the argument? Well, it is true that the Internet is difficult to censor but this is provided that the person is on the Internet in the first case. Some argue that censorship can bypass through an international telephone call. But this overlooks the economics of tele-communications. It is the less developed countries that have higher international telecommunication charges, even in absolute terms, than the developed countries. In relative terms, measured as a unit of hourly wages, the cost is even higher.

The common stereotype of a censor is that of someone who goes around with a black felt pen striking out words and pictures. On the Internet, such "pre-censorship" is not possible. Instead censorship is limited through controlling access and the behavior of users.

The 20 "enemies" regulate the conduct of users by having a central point of access. In most of these cases, there is only one Internet service provider. In China, public users have to register with the police to be an Internet subscriber.

In regulating individuals, governments often rely on the feat of punishment to restrain users. Of course, it is harder to enforce an act related to the Internet when it is such a personal medium and there is little or no evidence of any harm or effects from that act. In contrast, a murder usually leaves behind blood and the murder victim. And so all governments need to do to censor the Internet is to arrest a few people to set an example of the behavior it aims to discourage. But the chilling effect from the law is all that governments can hope to achieve.

IMPACT OF THE INTERNET

So what will make the Internet freer? First, it is important to recognise the impact of technology: there are unusual traits about the Internet. The Internet is an individual-empowering technology.

The history of computing, albeit brief, suggests that individual- or self-empowering technologies triumph over centre-empowering technologies. Early computers were centralized main frames. They were huge and expensive. The oft-repeated anecdote goes that when Thomas Watson of IBM was asked how many computers would likely be sold, he mentioned just five.

That indeed may be all that was needed because computing power was centered in a major hub. However, when the transistor and semiconductor chips revolutionized the computer industry, the power of computing was distributed to the individual. The computer industry really took off from 1980 when the personal computer was created. The world has not looked back since.

Closer to the example of the Internet, is the videotex. Of course one can now look back with amusement at the wrenching corporate pains of American newspaper firms like Knight-Ridder, the Los Angeles Times and AT&T that created the first videotex systems in America. Across the Atlantic, there were similar failures by government entities all across Europe. The only successful system, which ironically enough may become a drag in its entry into the Internet, is the French Minitel. In 1990, the French Minitel commanded more than 85 percent of the European Community's videotex market by revenue; the closest rival was Germany, which had less than a 5 percent share.

There are many reasons behind the dominance and success of Minitel. One of the interesting differences between the French Minitel and the other videotex systems around the world is its architecture: content was not centrally provided. Instead, content providers were encouraged to sell their content on Minitel on a revenue-sharing basis. In contrast, virtually all the other systems had a central content source with few alternative content providers. In other words, the most successful videotex system in the world was also the most decentralized. In brief, when it comes to information services, decentralization, not centralization, is more likely to lead to greater use.

In comparison with the Internet, any videotex system, including Minitel, looks centralized. Technology is not value-neutral; the Internet thrives on massive amounts of updated information. The videotex experiments have shown that it is difficult for any one or two or three sources to provide the volume and speed of information that would keep users hooked and coming back. Content provision has to be decentralized to interest the user.

This decentralization of content empowers the individual. And it is this empowerment that will ultimately make Asia freer.

What about censorship? Censorship has never been 100 percent effective of any medium in any country. There is always "leakage." On the Internet, the leakage is worse. This leakage, by definition, increases the space for freedom. The only way to reduce this leakage is to have tighter censorship. The question, however, is whether this is sustainable. Over the medium to long term, it is clearly not sustainable. It is not possible, or desirable, for governments to effectively censor the Internet. It would require too many censors. Computer personnel are scarce enough and to use them for censorship would literally be counter-productive.

The answer for governments who want to censor is that the censorship has to be selective. Just what areas to be selective in depends on the government. And here is the rub: by being forced to be selective, governments are forced to allow their citizens more space for expression.

Traditional media such as books, magazines and newspapers are more susceptible to censorship because of their physical nature; television and radio have central broadcasting nodes that are usually government-owned. What will limit the desire of governments to censor?

There are costs associated with censorship. These costs are more pronounced with the Internet than with traditional media. The cost of censorship today is the cost of not getting connected to the rest of the world. It is the Digital Divide writ global. It is likely to be even wider than any domestic digital divide. This price is too high for any government to bear even in the medium term. Therefore governments, almost by default, will offer Internet access albeit on their own terms.

Back in April 1996, Vietnam declared that it would not have allowed the Internet into the country. Understandably so, for the Internet is an American invention and it was not so long ago that they had fought the American War, which the rest of the world called the Vietnam War. But in November of that very same year, Vietnam organized an Internet day. This about-face is one example of how the information available through the Internet compels governments to allow their citizens to access the Net. Second, free market capitalism ultimately requires not just an individual empowered in economics but one empowered also in politics, society, culture, etc. - the entire gamut of life. One segment of life cannot be sealed off from another. They impinge on each other.

FORCES AGAINST

To be sure, there will be resistance—economic, cultural, social and political—and both active and inadvertent.

When India introduced a clause in its Information Technology Bill that would exempt Internet Service Providers from liability for third-party content, representatives of the Indian Music Industry and the National Association of Software and Service Companies wanted the clause deleted. After deliberation, the clause was allowed to stay with a condition attached that the ISPs would not be liable if they did not know of the offending third-party content.

In the short term, economics, especially in the realm of copyright, could crimp the forces of free expression. In the longer term, the resistance will be cultural, in the broad sense of the word. In the end, culture is stronger than technology

Participation in the computer world requires knowing English. At the time of writing, more than 80 percent of the content on the web is in English. For many parts of Asia, the need to read English would preclude most people from accessing much of the richness of the web. It is really useless to be able to access the web but be able to read nothing.

There are concerns that allowing multilingual URLs (uniform resource locators or domain name) would disrupt the viability of the Internet. The fear is that these multilingual domain names would be free from the central directory used to serve the 'Net.

Another issue with free speech is its divergent results. In the US, rumours are countered with rumours. In parts of Asia, rumours are acted upon, sometimes with deadly force. Witness the wholesale destruction of homes in Ambon, Indonesia, and of temples in India sparked off by rumour. Understandably, there are some grounds for caution.

TERRA INCOGNITA

This paper has not argued that unalloyed free speech is the ideal but that freer speech is better for citizenry than censored speech. The evidence is there empirically: Nobel Prize-winning economist Amartya Sen has observed that there have never been famines in countries with a democratic government and a functioning free press.

So even without the Internet, the world would have likely moved towards greater room for expression. The Internet is a catalyst to speed that up. But like any catalyst, how well it works depends on the compounds and elements it has to work with. And that is where the chemistry of Asia will be different from the West. And that is why the outcome will be different, too.

CHAPTER 5

Use of the Internet
for Democracy, Development and Empowerment In Nepal

VINAYA KASAJOO

ICT FROM ASIAN PERSPECTIVE

Taiwan and Hong Kong, China have become the two of the world's top three mobile telephone economies with more than 100 percent teledensity, and while in Nepal and Bangladesh there are only about 15 and 6 telephone lines respectively per 1000 people in each country, the lowest in the world. Asia Pacific, the home of over half of the world's population, is the most diverse region in the world with verities of cultures, languages, religion and people. There are dense cities and deserted areas. There are islands and the world's highest peaks. At the same time there are historic rivalries between the nations. But the diversity is most distinct in the digital divide among the countries of this continent.

According to the I.T.U.'s report "Asia-Pacific Telecommunication Indicators 2002", the region emerged as the world's largest telecommunication market in 2001. It is today home to over one-third of the world's telephone subscribers. In the last 10 years there have been immense and dramatic changes in telecommunications environment, in this continent, particularly with regard to the mobile phone. Even the least developed country like Cambodia has eight times more mobile phones than fixed-lines.

The report says that the Internet in Asia-Pacific has grown steadily. The region had some 160 million users at the end of 2001, accounting for one-third of the world total, and more than any other region. The region has more users of high-speed mobile Internet than the rest of the world put together.

Disparity among the Asian countries is not only the consequence of the physical diversity and inequality between the countries but also the result of centuries of western colonization. There is competition and also rivalry among the nations. They communicate between each other in the language and manner of their colonizers, something that is quite alien to the people of these countries. This causes misunderstanding and erodes self-confidence and self-respect; it makes them blind followers as well.

False history, subservient education system introduced during colonial period, the world economic order and the globalization of the market put together has made most of the Asian countries dependent on western economy, culture, social values and communication system. Asian skies are crowded with the communication satellites that broadcast western programs interfering continuously the life and culture of the Asian societies. In fact 'the global media has become new missionaries of global capitalism', as Herman and Mc Chesney said. However, its role in providing opportunities of interaction, and increasing the level of understanding among various nations, races, cultures and religions, is significant. Finding ways to make the media, both global and local, sustain and enhance cultural assets of the Asian countries is an important issue.

The need for regional cooperation and united action among the Asian countries is quite clear. They must discard the false pride based on religion, language, origin etc. created by the false colonial history. They should start fresh initiative to create vibrant Asian economy, culture and society with the help of new information and communication technologies.

NEPAL: A COUNTRY OF DIVERSITIES

Nepal is a small country of about 26 million people and an area of 147,181 sq km sandwiched between world's two population giants, China and India. It is a land of different kinds of diversities because of its unique geographical and geo-political situation. With a vertical span of 200 kilometers, north south, the altitude of the land ranges from 70 meters above sea level to the highest point on earth, Mount Everest (8500 meters). 17 % of its land is covered by snow-clad mountains while 64% land lies in mountain and hill area. Only 19 percent land is in the plain and fertile area, Terai, where 46% of the rural population lives.

While the country is stretched from east to west all the rivers originate from the Himalayan (snowy) mountain range in the north and flow southward making it difficult for the people to move east west, thus creating hundreds of small states, principalities and isolated, linguistic, ethnic and indigenous groups of people.

Because of the long autocratic rule for centuries the country remained isolated from rest of the world till 1951, when a multi-party democratic system was introduced that continued for a short period of ten years. Then the king introduced absolute monarchy, which continued for 30 years. A popular democratic movement ended the autocratic monarchy and established multiparty democracy within the framework of a constitutional monarchy in 1990. A Maoist insurgency, launched in 1996, has gained traction and is threatening to bring down the regime. In 2001, the Crown Prince massacred ten members of the royal family, including the king and queen, and then killed himself.

In October 2002, the new king dismissed the elected prime minister and his cabinet for "incompetence" after they dissolved the parliament and were subsequently unable to hold elections because of the ongoing insurgency. The country is now governed by the king and his appointed cabinet, which negotiated a cease-fire with the Maoist insurgents, who claim that there are two governments and two armies in the country. However, after seven months of cease fire and, third round of talk between the government and the Maoists, the Maoist unilaterally declared the end of cease-fire in September 2003. Situation of a kind of civil war and at the same time the political movement of constitutional parties to reinstall the parliament has created political limbo in the country and future of democracy seems uncertain.

Nepal is listed among the world's least developed countries. Its annual per capita income is around US$ 250. Most of the income of rural households (50 to 70%) is spent on food. The country is divided into 75 districts (administrative units). There are 58 towns, small and large, and around 4000 Village Development Committees, which elect local governments. However, there are no local governments elected since 2002. 85% of the total population lives in the rural area while only 15% live in urban areas.

Many Nepalese from rural areas work abroad, particularly India. Most of them work for low paid jobs. It is estimated that 25% households receive remittances.

COMMUNICATION IN NEPAL

Padam Maya Gurung, 34, who was undergoing jail sentence in a murder case in a prison situated in a hilly district, Tehrathum, suffered imprisonment for an extra six years because it took six years to deliver the court order to the prison authority. She has filed petition in the Dhankuta Appeal Court demanding compensation for excess incarceration of six years, more than the court verdict. The Supreme Court, based in Kathmandu had given verdict to release her in 1996 after the term of penalty. According to Gorkhapatra Daily (State owned newspaper), November 13, 2002 she was released from the jail only in May 2002, because it took six years to deliver the letter to this effect in the Tehrathum District Court.

Rolpa, a remote and hilly district, most affected by the Maoist rebellion, has neither electricity nor any form of print media. Battery-operated radio sets are the only source of news for the people. But, since the district administration banned the import and sale of batteries and ready-made packed food, the people of the district are deprived of listening to the radio (Kantipur Daily, September 18, 2002).

Nepal Communist Party (Maoist) Palpa district committee has put boxes in different parts of the district to collect peoples' opinion on peace process and their problems to be raised during peace talks with the government (Space Time Daily, March 5, 2003).

Besides ostensibly preparing for talks and sporadic exchanges of fire with the army the Maoists are currently exploring ways to air their message. They recently began a 'feasibility study' for a FM radio station and party activists have set up meetings with media professionals in Kathmandu, possibly with an eye on installation and broadcast training. The group seems to have the necessary funds, but lacks the technical and professional expertise to set up and run a radio station. The Maoists may find their biggest hurdle in acquiring license for the station. However, since they are an underground party, the issue of license may not be a formality (The Nepali Times # 158, 15-21 August, 2003).

Adverse geographical terrain; diverse culture, language and ethnic composition; lack of transportation; inadequate telecommunication infrastructure; political isolation and centuries-long feudal/autocratic administrative system, mass illiteracy (around 60%) and at the internal violence during last eight years, which has caused more than 8000 deaths and destruction of basic infrastructures, such as water, electricity and telecommunication, have badly effected the communication of Nepal. The postal service, which was started about two hundred years before and still carried by men on foot, is the most common and dependable form of communication for the rural people and the government offices at large.

Development of mass communication in Nepal, which started to take initial shape only after 1951, was interrupted for 30 years, during the autocratic Panchayat system. Although mass communication is the only sector that can claim to have developed most during the last 12 years of democracy, it is highly concentrated to a few urban centers, particularly in the Kathmandu, the capital of the country.

here is a vast imbalance of facilities between the capital and the rest of the country in the information and communication sector. Out of 23 million people only 2 million people live in the Kathmandu valley. But about half of the newspapers are published from Kathmandu. All five TV stations are based here. Out of 25 FM stations, 10 are in Kathmandu. According to the statistics of 2000 the national access to electricity, radio sets, TV sets and telephone line for households is 24.6%, 49.7%, 13.9% and 3.4% respectively. However the urban figure is 79.8%, 71%, 55.4% and 20.6% respectively and in rural area it is 16.5%, 46.6%, 7.8% and 0.9% respectively.

The mass media in Nepal is urban based, too politicized and elitist, highly polarized and sensationalist in character and has low circulation figures besides. As such the mass media have not been able to play an effective role in articulating the problems, reflecting the voice of the majority of the people, living particularly in rural areas, or safeguarding the citizens' rights and, in effect, strengthening democracy and enhancing development.

SIGNIFICANCE OF COMMUNITY MEDIA

The mass media has failed to play effective role in the life of the majority of the people who live in the rural and remote areas. The global media has no relevance or use for the majority of the people, who live below poverty line. Indigenous, traditional and community media are the most widely used form of information and communication system. Modern tools of communication, such as radio, television, cable network, and print media have started to play role in the communities now.

The idea of community media is to establish communication via radio, television, print and the Internet of, for and by the people. These would be citizen-controlled media for non-commercial and social development purposes. Varieties of communication tools, from wall newspapers to the Internet, have been tested here, and some of them have proved quite effective. Wall newspapers, community audio tower, rural newspaper run by barefoot journalists, and community/cooperative FM radio stations are some of the successful models in South Asia tested in Nepal. Now telecenters and cyber cafes have started to play the role of community media. It has a great potential in the Nepalese context.

Understanding communities and teaching communities members to amplify their own voices is important. Media developed in foreign places are aimed at selling products. People need to create their own media for their own uses and development. People need to be media literate so that they can help children discover the motives behind most commercial media rather than blindly succumb to its magic. Media literacy requires the analysis, critic, deconstruction and the creation of a media. That is why community media initiatives are so important for communities living in rural areas as they are prone to the harmful effects of the global/satellite media.

INTERNET OBSESSION

The Nepalese media, both the printed and electronic variety, were the first to cover the news of the inauguration of the first interactive religious website by the Nepalese queen on 19 May 2003. It was the first time that a royal dignitary such as the queen had inaugurated a website (www.shripa shupatinath.org) .

Two more websites were also launched on the same day, this was also covered by the media. Minister of Culture, Tourism and Civil Aviation inaugurated a website of his ministry (www.tourism.gov.np) while Miss Nepal launched the website of the World Wildlife Fund of Nepal (www. wwfnepal.org.np) .

Dozens of websites are launched every week, but most of them remain unnoticed not only by the media but also by the people for whom they are made. In July 2003 the royal palace launched its website, www.nepal monarchy.gov.np. Almost all ministries of the government have websites. With the support of UNDP and other development organizations some of the municipalities, village committees and nongovernmental organizations have created websites. Indeed the attraction of and enthusiasm for adopting new information technology is continuously increasing in Nepal.

IT CAPACITY IN NEPAL

The number of fixed and mobile telephone lines, have reached around 400,000 in Nepal. Most significantly more than 68% of the telephone lines (including mobile phones) are distributed in the Kathmandu valley. While the national teledensity is 1.4%, it is 23% in Kathmandu and 0.14% in the rest of the country. 60% of the villages have no access to telephones.

Out of the total capacity of 70 thousand mobile phones (introduced two years ago), around 34 thousand mobile phones are distributed in the Kathmandu valley. There are about 30,000 Internet account holders/customers in the country and it is estimated that about 200,000 people use email and Internet. Out of 18 Internet Service Providers (ISP) 15 are providing service. However, all of them are based in Kathmandu. Very few of them are providing service in urban centers outside the valley.

Although the government has announced that the private sector should be involved in the telecommunication service, no significant change has been seen. The government has not allowed private the sector to operate in full-fledged telecommunication services.

IT USAGE

The Nepalese used the Internet, for the first time, as a credible and easy source of information during the dreadful royal massacre on June 1, 2001 to get news that they could not get from the mainstream media. That was the first time people outside Nepal browsed the Nepalese website to its utmost capacity.

There are lots of inconsistencies and contradictions in the development of Nepal. People of the hill and mountain areas of Nepal used airplanes and helicopters before they saw vehicles. Similarly people who had never read newspapers or listened to radios are enjoying satellite television powered by solar energy. This leapfrog development can be experienced in the Information Technology (IT) sector too. People who until recently barely had made a telephone call or seen a computer are now benefiting from the Internet.

It seems that people have suddenly found a miraculous pot in the form of the Internet to fulfill all kinds of wishes. Students, researchers and intellectuals have found that there is no better alternative to IT for increasing the dimensions of their knowledge. Human right activists, development workers and social advocates have been using it for increasing numbers of supporters and raising funds. Businessmen have realized that they can increase their profits through IT. Professionals have benefiting gaining a wide rang of contacts. Even the farmers and craftsmen, who live in rural areas, have got new in opportunities by selling products on international markets. Local products are thus getting global markets. Political leaders, decision makers and bureaucrats have realized that IT is the most effective tool for empowering people, delivering services, promoting good governance and strengthening democracy.

Despite the adverse situation and poor telecommunication status of the country there is a great enthusiasm among the youth and IT professionals who have worked to promote the development of IT in the country from the beginning. As a result, Nepal is gradually heading towards a state where IT is no more a luxury, but a necessity. Development agencies and civil society are already utilizing IT and the policy-makers, bureaucrats and politicians are realizing that poorer the nation, the greater the importance of IT. IT is capable of promoting development for the rural poor in a country like Nepal.

The major role of IT in Nepal is mainly as a communication technology rather than as an information processing or production technology, particularly in the rural and remote communities.

Areas where the Internet can be used are increasing every day. INGOs and NGOs are at the forefront in benefiting from the Internet. Within a short period, the use of ICT has increased in many sectors including government, civil societies and the economic sector. Other sectors such as health, education, business, tourism, governance and mass communication are also using the Internet. It has increased the efficiency and capacity of the organizations and benefited people in various ways.

MEDIA AND ONLINE JOURNALISM

Dialogue within and among people, communities and different institutions, which is so important for strengthening democracy, enhancing development and empowering people, is increasing rapidly with the increase of communication tools such as telephone, fax, FM radio, email, and Internet. Nepalese mass media is using IT in various ways for accessing and increasing sources of information, speeding up the flow of information and getting feed back. Online journalism has made it quite easy for people abroad to get online news about Nepal and vice versa. The overall meaning of journalism is changing since anybody with a computer and a telephone line can be a journalist and produce his/her own media or broadcast voice and video through the Internet. Press Council Nepal, which monitors the code of conduct of journalists, is documenting all the newspapers digitally.

DEMOCRACY AND GOVERNANCE

A strong democracy demands a constant and vibrant interaction between government and civil society, between the administration and the common people. The Internet provides opportunities for a two-way dialogue between the state and its citizens. It affects the decisions of the peoples' elected representatives and policy makers makes the local and central governments, and public organizations accountable, transparent, and more sensible, and it reduces corruption. It also makes government services and other organizations services more effective and responsible.

All the government ministries, departments, corporations and district offices are going to have their own websites and their databases are going to be linked by a national network within five years. Other organs of the state, such as the Judiciary, the Parliament, the Election Commission, the Human Rights Commission, the Bureau of Statistics etc. have their websites and databases on computers. Anybody can send emails about corruption by public servants or the peoples' representative to the Commission for Investigation of Abuse of Authority (see www.akhtiyar.org.np).

There are many websites dealing with the human rights situation of the country, which give updated information on violation of human rights to human right activists around the world (see www.insec.org.np, www.cvict.org.np, www.cehurdes.org.np, and www.cwin-nepal.org).

INTERNET FACILITY FOR MPS

Free Internet and telephone facilities were provided to the members of the parliament with the objectives of popularizing new information technology and increase the dimensions of knowledge. Since the majority of constituencies did not have telephone and Internet connections it was unthinkable that a MPs would use the Internet as a tool for interacting with their voters or getting consensus for any bill tabled in the parliament. However, as far as the interaction between the MPs and their voters was concerned the radio program "Phone in with the Parliamentarians" was quite popular and successful to some extent for making the peoples' representatives realize their responsibilities and empowering the voters.

TELECENTERS IN RURAL AREAS

A pilot project to install 15 rural telecenters in 15 different VDCs in 9 Districts is already under way, under the joint management of Ministry Of Science and Technology and National Information Technology Centre and the UNDP-funded ICTs for Development programmes. Each telecenter will provide telephony and Internet access, plus specialised local content, which is being developed for the purpose. The aim of the project is to establish 1500 such sponsored telecenters within next five years.

DISTRICT INFORMATION AND DOCUMENTATION CENTRES

The UNDP-funded Local Governance Programme is setting up 30 District Information and Documentation Centres (DIDC), each with a networked computer. These will be linked to the Ministry of Local Government. The project is closely linked with the new development approach of social mobilisation to form Community Based Organisations. The DIDCs will be both a resource and an outlet for the CBOs, providing a channel whereby they can express their needs. A different UNDP-funded programme, PDDP (Participatory District Development Programme), is providing similar facilities to a similar number of other Districts.

A current proposal, awaiting approval, is for the Japanese to support the NTC to install pilot multipurpose community telecenters (MCT) in 10 VDCs in the Kathmandu Valley, each are 2-3 hours' drive from Kathmandu and with population of over 4,000 people. The purpose is to develop a sustainable model for MCTs, trying out different approaches of charging and comparing MCTs with simple public call offices. Each MCT will have 2 phones, 1 computer with modem, 1 fax machine, 1 printer and uninterruptible power supply.

Nepal is also using a geographical information system (GIS) in 66 districts to assist planning in various sectors. It has also started using a global positioning system (GPS). The Internet is also used for environmental conservation initiatives within and outside the country.

A District Treasury Control project has linked computers in 64 Districts and major municipalities to central government. This has made cash management faster and more transparent.

EDUCATION

Educational institutions are increasingly using IT, and an initiative to start distance learning has begun recently. Some of the books and documents, including textbooks, in the Nepalese language are available on the Internet. People are using e-libraries. Students browse websites to seek an appropriate college with the right syllabus, scholarships and jobs. Thousands of students and their guardians outside the capital have started browsing school and college examination results on the Internet, which were not possible to see three years ago.

HEALTH

The HealthNet provides online access for doctors and nurses to international health databases and Nepalese health information. A Local Area

Network connects more than 70 terminals on and near the Tribhuvan University Teaching Hospital campus, providing direct access for on-site staff. Doctors who are further away can access HealthNet using a secure dial-up method. HealthNet provides weeklong training for doctors who are not yet familiar with computers, the Internet and search methods. People can donate blood and request for blood donations through website, www.bloodmembers.com. Telemedicine has a vast scope and utility in Nepal.

Commerce: e-commerce has started up in Nepal but it has not been able to develop in comparison to other countries because of the lack of cyber laws, which is in the offing now. The tourism industry is using the Internet to expand its business around the world. Some websites are demonstrating handicrafts of rural craftsmen, thus helping them sell their product on international markets.

AGRICULTURE

There are websites, which provide information about agricultural products and on the market price of produce in different towns of the country. AgriPriceNepal.com is a pioneer Nepali website on agricultural market information for Nepal, jointly hosted by the Rural-Urban Partnership Programme, the Agro Enterprise Centre and the Federation of Nepalese Chambers of Commerce and Industry. Subscribers can get the latest price and source information for more than 150 agricultural commodities of 18 major markets in Nepal.

IT-based businesses such as call centers, cyber cafes, medical transcription, digitization of maps and documents; software production etc. have started up during the last five years. Consequently considerable numbers of youth are attracted to train for and join the IT-based professions.

Art and Literature: There are some websites, such as www.spinybab bler.org, www.aarohantheatre.org, www.mpp.org.np, www.thopathopa.com, and www.kasajoo.com, which provide art, literature and news on literary activities. Some of them are in Nepali and others in different national languages. There are Nepali literary magazines originating in Nepal and abroad in the Nepali language.

CULTURE, TRADITION AND RELIGION

With the help from some websites Nepalese living in foreign countries can now perform religious, cultural and traditional rites, rituals and ceremonies.

DEVELOPMENT ORGANIZATIONS

International donor communities have been using the Internet in Nepal for a long time. They have also supported national and regional non-governmental organizations to establish their own websites. Although these websites are not used so much within the country due to language and technological constraints they have been quite useful as a tool of advocacy for social change in Nepal and for raising funds for projects which help uplift the life of the people. It has been very easy for the international development organizations based outside Nepal to understand the reality of the country; evaluate the seriousness of problems; realize the needs of the grassroots, identify the areas which need intervention and decide which plans and projects should address the problems. It has also helped them to monitor and evaluate projects. Similarly people from any part of the world can support vulnerable communities.

CHALLENGES

Internet fidelity is increasing in Nepal and so are increasingly the number of networks and websites. However, it seems that the target audience of most of the websites and their promoters is not within the country. They are meant for international visitors, who can communicate in the English language. For example Nepal's most used online news www.nepalnews.com is visited by around 40 thousand people daily all over the world. Out of all visitors only 15 percent are from Nepal, according to the editor. The present telecommunication infrastructure and the other facilities necessary for using the Internet are quite limited. It is estimated that less than 1% of the population use email and the Internet while the total number of Internet account holders is around 30,000 (less than 0.14%).

Language is another great barrier for accessing and using computers for the majority of the Nepalese. Historically, Nepal was the only country in

South Asia, which was not colonized by a western power. It was isolated for centuries. English was and still is one of the official languages in the South Asian countries. Consequently very few Nepalese can communicate in English, which is the dominating language on the Internet. Until the software that runs computer programmes, are made in the Nepali language using the Nepali font it is impossible for more than 90% of the Nepalese population to operate computers and browse the Internet by themselves.

Dr. Michael L. Dertouzon, engineer, inventor, theoretician and director of the Laboratory for Computer Science at the Massachusetts Institute of Technology, has predicted many ways the information revolution would affect human lives, he may also help us understand the basic reality about the use of IT in Nepal, Indeed he stated that:

> *Bill sees this expanding world of network as an opportunity for poor people to sell their wares, get educated participate in the world marketplace and pull themselves up from poverty. I see the exact same thing with a time scale of 15 years —and only, if we help.*
>
> *I learnt it from Nepal. A while ago, I had this naïve assumption that I could go to Nepal, obtain computers and training for the Nepalese and get them to have a 20 percent jolt in the G.N.P. But here is what I found out: Only 30 percent of the Nepalese are literate. Of that 30 percent only 10 percent speak English. Even if I got someone to provide every one of them with a computer with communications, what could they do with them? They have no skills to sell...To get people to do this, I would have to educate them, and people don't get educated overnight ... So, 15 years. From this and other experiences, I've concluded that the information revolution, if left to its own devices, will mean that the rich are going to buy more computers, be more productive and become richer, and the poor will not be able to do that and will stand still. History teaches us that whenever the gap between rich and poor increases, we have all kinds of troubles.* (Claudia Dreifus, The Kathmandu Post, Cyberpost, September 29, 1999)

Energy is an important aspect for using computer. Electricity is available mainly in urban areas. It is very difficult to supply main line electricity to rural households, which are scattered far and wide. Denmark is significantly supporting the development of alternative energy in Nepal. More than 25 thousand households belonging to 1100 Village Development Committees are using solar energy thanks to the alternative energy project. Solar energy is used mostly for watching TV and listening to radio while a few of them also are used for running computers. The target is to set up 52000 solar power sets within next five years. The project has proved useful and effective for increasing communication facilities in rural and remote areas. Developed countries must increase their support to such projects, including wind power and small hydroelectricity projects, which directly benefit the rural people.

There is a great digital divide inside the country, between the urban and rural areas, and also between the Kathmandu valley and rest of the country. More than 95 percent of the websites originate from the capital city. The number of Internet users is not increasing at the same ratio as websites. The number of Internet account holders is estimated to increase 20 to 30 percent every year.

All the Internet Service Providers depend on the Nepal Telecommunication Corporation (NTC) to connect up with the end users. Apart from the Internet charges the customers have to pay the telephone charge at the same rate as that of the voice telephone, which is quite costly in comparison to other countries. At the same time NTC also provides Internet service.

Problems regarding the access to Internet, particularly in rural areas, are related to unreliable and variable power supply, low bandwidth leading to slow connections, lack of local software and hardware support, lack of awareness among local people of facilities offered, poor location, inadequate opening hours and inadequate dedicated management.

Lack of laws regarding electronic transaction has hindered the development of e-commerce and export of software, which has already shown vast potentiality in the country.

Various measures should be taken to overcome the barriers concerning access and use of IT, such as, adverse geographical condition, poverty, inadequate telecommunication infrastructure, high illiteracy, unfriendly Internet and telephone tariffs, domination of the English language in IT, the monopoly of the Nepal Telecommunication Corporation (NTC), unfriendly licensing policy and high fees and taxes for Internet businesses (small entrepreneur), lack of electricity and diversity of language etc. It is necessary to formulate relevant policies and laws, adopt appropriate technology, utilize external assistance and conduct training. However, the main challenge seems to be more socio-cultural rather than physical.

The fear of the cost and the mastering of new technology is not as great as the fear of loosing control over the existing knowledge/information system. For example, the bureaucrats in the government offices usually dislike both the idea of keeping all the official documents on the computer and networking within the ministry, department or the office. Hence on the ministries websites we see biographies of ministers, messages from ministers, secretaries and the head of the departments instead of the relevant data. This is true not only in the case of the government offices, but this kind of media hierarchy is prevalent in many organizations, NGOs and within families.

Overcoming this socio-cultural or mental barrier seems to be the greatest challenge, which many Asian countries including Nepal have to address. Once this mental barrier is crossed all other barriers such as policy, law, monopoly, tariff, access, rural connectivity etc. can be overcome. This is a problem for most of the Asian countries and we should find the solution ourselves.

RECOMMENDATIONS

Only small parts of the societies in South Asia have access to the Internet and other new means of communication. There exist serious inequalities in these countries which constrain the use of ICT- based information by the majority of the people.

It is not possible to make all the citizens capable of using the Internet or quickly make them computer literate. To overcome the barriers there is a distinct role to be played by intermediaries that connect the people to the technology by providing them with IT related services and enabling them to use the Internet. Therefore the intermediaries, such as community tele-centers, cyber cafes, local governments with IT facilities, ISPs etc. should be given incentives and their role in the communities should be increased. At the same time it is important to increase the access for the people to use IT by implementing IT awareness programs and organizing different levels of trainings on a large scale.

As theechnology is advancing, the gap between the information haves and have-nots is also widening. The digital divide is increasing not only between the nations, and within the countries, but also within the communities and between different sexes and races and ethnic groups. IT may therefore have a greater role to play by giving voice to the deprived vulnerable sex, race and groups of people. It is important to make them information providers rather than information recipients.

Since women are the most underprivileged/ deprived class in Nepal in all sectors of society it is important to focus on increasing the communication technology capacity for women in, both traditional and new.

One of the main strategies of the international community for supporting the least developed countries should be to increase the number of people getting access to the Internet and the new technologies. This may involve supporting the following measures:

- Putting pressure on national governments to create a legal and economic environment in order to encourage the private sector to provide complete and independent telecommunication services.

- Development of a telecommunication infrastructure in remote and rural areas.

- Support to subsidize the costs of communication satellites. This is important for land locked and mountainous countries like Nepal.

- Improving the bandwidth provided by satellite communication technology in order to supply the necessary/appropriate bandwidth for broadband and Internet connectivity.

- Promotion of alternative/community media initiatives, both electronic and printed media.

- Subsidizing alternative energy projects.

Whether people are ready or not it is true that IT is a reality now even for a country like Nepal where the tele-dencity has not crossed 1.5 percent. It is also true that the poorer the nation, the greater the importance of IT. In comparison to neighboring countries the situation of landlockedness and scarcity of physical resources makes IT especially important for Nepal. IT has a great potential for empowering people, and empowerment of the people is the key for strengthening democracy and enhancing development.

CHAPTER 6

Indigenous Peoples' Experiments with ICT
as a Tool for Political Participation and other Socio-Cultural Struggles in Sabah, Malaysia

JENIFER LASIMBANG AND DEBBIE GOH

INTRODUCTION

In barely a decade, the Internet has become an integral part of routine communication activities of governments, businesses and the general public in many countries (Colle & Roman, 2001). So rapid and pervasive is the growth and use of computers that countries begin to fear a digital divide between technological haves and have-nots. The exponential growth of telecenters across the globe has been initiated by government and non-government groups to help those who cannot afford it or have no access to computers and the Internet enabling them to become part of the information society. This drive to provide those who are technologically marginalized with IT access lies in the belief that information and communication technology (ICT) is the key to the social and economic development of these places and the people. Rogers & Shukla (2001) listed the potential of ICT, where ICT:

1. connects disadvantaged people with societal decision-makers so that their voices may be heard in the agenda-setting process.

2. empower people and communities to determine their own futures through developing self-efficacy and collective efficacy

3. provides accurate information about social problems and their possible solutions.

The Internet is regarded as a revolutionary liberating force, empowering an individual with the ability to participate fully and knowledgeably in politics. It creates new ways for citizens to demand accountability from their government and in the use of public resources (Human Development Report, 2001). Bikson and Panis (1995) found that access to ICT influenced opportunities of communities to participate effectively in a range of economic, social and civic activities. Kruegar (2002) further found that given equal access, the Internet shows the potential to bring new individuals into the political process, and that those without resources traditionally needed for civic participation (civic skills, money and free time) are more likely to benefit from being involved online.

It is no surprise then that communities that have been politically marginalized have chosen ICT as its champion for greater emancipation, democracy, and political influence.

Indigenous people's strife for self-determination includes the right to control their own economies, determine their form of self-government, and uphold indigenous political systems, and form alliances and federations with other indigenous peoples (Nicholas, 1996). Strategies that they use to attain their goals include creating awareness of their situation and seeking the support of the international community, both of which can be efficiently facilitated using ICT. Many indigenous groups around the world have thus begun using the Internet to establish effective linkages to further indigenous peoples' development and to promote indigenous rights (Gigler, 2001).

INDIGENOUS PEOPLES IN SABAH, MALAYSIA

Sabah occupies the northern portion of the island of Borneo and covers an area of 27,800 sq miles and it is the second largest of the 13 states in Malaysia. Sabah, together with Sarawak, makes up East Malaysia, which is separated from Peninsular Malaysia by about 1, 200 miles of the South China Sea (Lasimbang, 1996).

Indigenous communities make up about 60 percent of the estimated 2.6 million (based on the 2000 Census) total population of Sabah. They comprise more than 30 ethnic groups; speak more than 50 languages and 80 dialects (Tongkul, 2002).

The indigenous peoples of Sabah have been struggling with the government over numerous issues for decades, including land ownership and control of

(Above) women and children using ICT in Sabah , Malasia.

(Below) Women and participating in a discussion. (Photo: DoreenLasimbang)

natural resources. About 70 per cent live in rural or forested villages where basic infrastructure such as electricity, telephone lines and postal services are still absent. They thus have few means of getting sufficient updated information on the Malaysian general elections, government processes, and changes in land ownership rights, land titles, and forest development that affect them directly. They only have few means of contacting state or federal government officials. The lack of information and communication facilities results in indigenous communities being poorly organized and unfamiliar with political processes, preventing them gaining their indigenous rights.

ICT can be a panacea for greater accessibility to the state and federal government, and promote political participation by indigenous peoples in Malaysia. The need for ICT to reach Malaysia' indigenous communities is further enhanced by the Malaysian government's move to offer its services online.

SETTING UP COMMUNITY TECHNOLOGY CENTERS (CTC)

In order to create opportunity for indigenous communities of Sabah to have access to ICT, a pilot project was set up in two communities in March 2003 in order to create a CTC. A CTC is a community-owned center where a network of volunteers provides training for the community by using donated ICT resources with the hope that the community will be able to use ICT as a tool to achieve its social, cultural, economic and political goals (Gurstein, 2000).

In order to establish the two pilot centers the developer:

1. established a connection with PACOS Trust, a non-profit organization.

2. identified two communities to implement the pilot project, namely, Nampasan and Terian.

3. successfully acquired donations from individuals.

4. held discussions with both communities.

5. set up CTCs in both communities and presented donations.

6. conducted training sessions.

7. collected the communities' evaluations.

Building the CTC in Terain. The community is also working hard fund raising.

Presentation of the laptop donated to the Terian community. Photos Adrian Lasimbang

Establishing ties to a non-profit organization in Sabah

A local non-profit organization based in Sabah, PACOS Trust, is an established community-based, volunteer organization with a vision "to create peaceful and united indigenous communities equipped with the knowledge and skills to manage resources and opportunities to support a comfortable life" (PACOS website).

The connection with PACOS is very important for this project because PACOS's Management Committee helped to identify two communities, namely Nampasan and Terian, where the pilot project was implemented. The partnership was very fruitful and many volunteers were recruited through PACOS's network.

Through discussions with the Management Committee of PACOS Trust, an agreement to establish the community informatics (CI) program in their organization was reached. The main objective of the CI program was to assist an indigenous community in establishing and managing its CTC. A website was developed to give information about the CI program. Some individuals also came forward and donated a laptop, a PC and several printers to start up the two CTCs. The computers and printers now belong to the communities.

Discussing the pilot project with the communities

The pilot project was discussed with the parents, children, and leaders of the communities. Some voiced their concern about how the new technology would affect their children's lives. One concerned mother said, *"My husband told me, if you know how to use a computer, then you can see dirty pictures."* It was important for the developer to explain to parents and the whole community that children needed to be supervised and monitored when using a computer.

A very vocal 56-year old woman said, *"I heard old ladies like us are not welcome to these training sessions."* After explaining to her that the training workshops are for the whole community, she attended the first session, accompanied by her son. They never missed any of the training sessions and were one of the earliest to arrive.

At the end of the discussion with the Terian community, some decisions were made:

- It was decided to temporarily place the computer and other equipment in the primary school office because the community had plans to build an "information center." One community leader told the developer that having a computer in that center would be "wonderful."

- Other leaders from neighboring communities were there and heard about the project. They asked if they could have something similar in their community.

After the discussions, it was concluded that the Terian and Nampasan communities had expressed their interest in the pilot project and that they now were ready to participate in the project.

Setting up the CTCs

Setting up Nampasan's CTC was relatively easy. Not only was the community very receptive to the idea of having their own CTC, but also an immediate location to house the CTC was found. The community had a training center with an office, which was turned into a CTC over two weekends. Members of the community helped the developer to rearrange the furniture in the office to suit the nature of the training sessions.

There was an existing PC and printer, and additional resources were easily acquired by means of donations from members of the community. In the span of two weeks, the center became the computer-training center for the whole community. A small fee was collected for the CTC's maintenance.

In no time at all, a number of community members came to work on the computers. They wrote a book, edited documents, and designed wedding invitation cards.

However, setting up Terian's CTC was very challenging. Although the whole community was very interested, there was no place to house the CTC. During the dialogue session with the community, a few people were very vocal and enthusiastic about the center, and were immediately identified as the "champions" of this project (Roman and Colle, 2002). The community planned to set up an "information center" hence the idea of setting up a CTC was found to be very appropriate for their plan. For a month, the community worked hard to find volunteers in the village and to start the construction of their CTC.

Currently, Nampasan's CTC was completed and operational containing three PCs, two laptops, one printer, and one big TV screen for training sessions. Terian's CTC is under construction but the community already has one laptop and one printer donated by kind individuals.

Introducing Solar-powered computers to the Terian community

The developer investigated the best source of power for the CTC in Terian since there was no electricity in Terian village. The developer approached Mr Adrian Lasimbang – an experienced resource person in the area of renewably energy for advice. Adrian proposed to set up, test, and install a solar-powered computer system for the Terian community. He then volunteered to implement this system.

The solar-powered computer system was tested before being brought to the remote village of Terian. It was initially set up outside the Nampasan CTC for testing. The setting up process and the testing took two days. Adrian had all the components ready, i.e., the solar panels, battery, controller, and inverter and assembled them together on the first day. The second day was a sunny day; the battery became fully charged thus the system worked successfully.

Transporting the components

A group of volunteers came forward to transport the solar system components, laptop, and the printer to Terian. However, the battery and the solar panels were not transported during the first trip because there were not enough volunteers. The existing solar panels and batteries in the primary school were used temporarily instead. The journey was a six-hour hike into the Crocker Range.

The group of volunteers arrived late in the afternoon, and the community – children and the adults alike, greeted them. The technology champions of Terian came to inform the volunteers that the installation was planned to take place the next day.

Adrian and his technical assistant (another volunteer) installed the solar system components after school the next day in the school's office. A careless mistake by another volunteer caused a short circuit in the system and consequently the controller was burnt. Fortunately, it was a non-critical

*The solar-powered computer system was installed for testing in its temporary location –
the community's primary school Photo: Jenifer Lasimbang*

*A solar-powered computer system was set up for testing outside Nampasan CTC. Photo:
Jannie Lasimbang*

*Adrian explaining how the system works. He trained the local champions in the basic
maintenance of the solar-powered computer system. Photo: Jenifer Lasimbang*

component so it still worked. After two hours, the whole system was set up and running.

TRAINING SESSIONS

After the system was successfully installed, Adrian carefully briefed the community technology champions on the maintenance of the system. Each of the components was described, and a simple sketch of the system was created for the community's reference.

All training sessions were conducted in the local language by the developer. Computer terms in the indigenous language were developed with the help of members of the community.

Training the Nampasan Community

Most of the people in the Nampasan community had basic computer skills, and a number of households had computers at home so they came to the training session to upgrade their computer skills. Community members were charged a minimal training fee, (RM 10 – approx. US$2.50) to be used for maintenance of the Nampasan CTC. Each training session was hands-on and consisted of five participants. Customized training was also provided to community members.

Training the Terian Community

A five-day training session was conducted during the developer's visit to Terain village in July 2003. Community leaders supported and participated in the training, and some of the parents who accompanied their children to the training session stayed and attended as well because they live an hour from the training venue and because the training was conducted at night. These sessions were done free of charge.

POST-EVALUATION

After the training sessions, community members gave a lot of feedback to the developer. Nine-year old Aril and his mother thought that the training sessions were established "to conduct computer training sessions so that the whole Terian community would know how to use the computer".

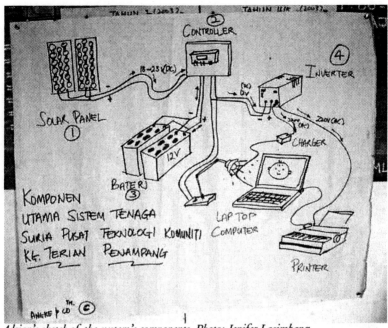

Adrian's sketch of the system's components. Photo: Jenifer Lasimbang

First training session in the Nampasan cummunity. People were crowding round despite only five people were allowed per session. Photo Jenifer Lasimbang

The Terian community — most people were looking at a computer for the first time in their life. Photo: Doreen Lasimbang

Children of the Terian community. Learning to use a mouse. Photo: Doreen Lasimbang

The feedback received from the community members was very helpful for improving the training sessions and for future implementation of the project. Continuous feedback from the community will be useful for the developer of the project.

STRATEGIES

Improving current CTC facilities
The current CTC facilities in Terian and Nampasan need to be improved so as to support Internet access. As for volunteers, they need to continue working with the communities to find the most cost-effective way to provide Internet access for the communities and conduct more training sessions in order to improve the community's computer skills.

Replicating the pilot project in other indigenous communities
It is hoped that this pilot project can be replicated in other indigenous communities in Sabah and maybe even around the world. There is similar work being done around the globe, and findings and lessons learned from this project can be incorporated into current and future efforts.

Creating indigenous content
The next step for the two communities is to find ways to use the current facilities to create indigenous content, e.g., document folk songs and stories, traditional medicine, and traditional knowledge for publishing. The documentation of an indigenous culture and knowledge is part of preserving its identity.

Training modules in the local language
The community will be more comfortable learning a new technology in their local language; in other words, information will be more effectively conveyed through the local language.
The developer prepared the computer-training module in the indigenous language for the Terian and Nampasan community. Therefore, there is a great need for comprehensive training modules in the indigenous languages.

Future funding
It is hoped that there will be more funding and support from the government, organizations, and individuals in the future. There is a need to find donors to set up new CTCs and improve the current CTCs.

The Terian community were very receptive of the CTC pilot project. Photo: Doreen
Lasimbang

Rina helping her sister Risa, who was holding her note book, to type her story into the
computer. Photo: Adrian Lasimbang

Training module in the indigenous language. Photo: Jenifer Lasimbang

Service-Research

This project could be classified as service-research in that it has combined community service and research. The community benefited from the training and documentation that was part of the research project. (Lazar and Norcio, 2002). The project built relationships between universities and local communities. Service research is a way for universities to contribute to the local communities. The expertise and services provided by the universities through their research projects enabled the communities to improve their skills in using new technology.

CONCLUSION

It is limited what can be achieved from such a pilot project. However the project proved that it was possible to provide two secluded villages without electricity with a computer technology center and successfully train villagers, young and old, in using computer technology, including e-mail and Internet. This enables the communities to communicate with government agencies via emails and gain crucial up-to-date information from government websites.

REFERENCES

Bikson, T. K., & Panis, C. W. (1995). "Computers and connectivity: current trends. In Anderson *et al*, (Eds.), *Universal Access to Email: Feasibility and Societal Implications.* RAND.

Colle, R. D., & Roman, R. R. (2001). "Telecenter environment in 2002". In *The Journal of Development Communication*, 12, 1-15.

Gigler, B. S. (2001). *Empowerment through the Internet: Opportunities and challenges for indigenous peoples.* Retrieved September 18, 2003, from http://www.developmentgateway.org/node/133831/sdm/docview?docid=627641

Gurstein, M. (2000). *Community Informatics: Enabling Communities with Information and Communications Technologies.* Hershey, PA: Idea Group Publishing

Kruegar, B. S. (2002). "Assessing the potential of Internet political participation in the United States: A resource approach". *American Politics Research*, 30, 476-498.

Lasimbang, Jannie (1996). "The Indigenous Peoples of Sabah". In Nicholas, C. & Singh, R. (Eds.). *Indigenous Peoples of Asia: Many Peoples, One Struggle.* Bangkok, Thailand: Asia Indigenous Peoples Pact.

Lazar, J., and Norcio, A. F., (2002). "Service-Research Partnership: Research Projects that Help Bridge the Digital Divide". In Lazar (Ed.) *Managing IT/Community Partnerships in the 21st Century.* Hershey, PA: Idea Group Publishing

Nicholas, C. (1996). "A common Struggle: Regaining Control". In Nicholas, C., Singh, R. (Eds.). *Indigenous Peoples of Asia: Many Peoples, One Struggle.* Bangkok, Thailand: Asia Indigenous Peoples Pact.

Roman, R. & Colle, R. D. (2002). *Themes and Issues in Telecentre Sustainability.* Institute for Development Policy and Management, University of Manchester. Retrieved August 20, 2003, from http://idpm.man.ac.uk/publications/wp/di/di_wp10.pdf

Rogers, E. M., and Shukla, P. (2001). "The role of telecenters in development communication and the digital divide". *The Journal of Development Communication*, 12, 26-31.

Tongkul, F. (2002). *Traditional Systems of Indigenous Peoples of Sabah, Malaysia: Wisdom Accumulated Through Generations.* Sabah, Malaysia: PACOS Trust.

United Nations Development Program. (2001). *Human Development Report 2001.* Retrieved September 18, 2003, from http://hdr.undp.org/reports/global/2001/en/

CHAPTER 7

Democracy and Virtual Politics
Young People, the Internet and Political Participation

JOHANNES ANDERSEN

THE INTERNET AND POLITICS

The Internet is an aspect of everyday life for contemporary youth. Politics, on the other hand, is not. Many young people regard politics as something that is to be taken care of by others, with the very exception of voting. The youth of today is therefore the segment of the population that is relatively least interested in politics (Andersen 2003, Levinsen 2003). In the meantime, the increasing focus on the general democratic potential of the Internet has stimulated hope that interaction between youth, the Internet and politics can result in greater interest in politics – and ultimately result in increased political participation – among young people.

The foundation for this hope is a number of assumptions pertaining to the democratic potential of the Internet relating to a number of areas (e.g. Wilhelm 2000, Dahlgren 2001, Sparks 2001, Gimmler 2001, Kaare Nielsen 2002, Hoff 2002):

a.   The Internet makes it possible for an increasing number of citizens to raise political questions that they find to be of interest for the political public sphere. Critical questions can be addressed to authorities, focus given to cases regarded to be of central significance for society, and prompt reaction is possible. In this light, the Internet is an optimal forum for political mobilisation, particularly for young people, of whom most are on the Net on a daily basis.

b. The Internet provides access to more information about politics and political questions. Authorities provide access to documents; researchers provide access to their results, parties to their ideas, etc. In other words, political communication has been increased by the Internet, which ought to mean that young people should chance upon abundant amounts of information with political significance while on the Net. Similarly, the copious information offers greater insight in politics. In brief, young people are challenged and informed about politics by going on the Net.

c. The Internet constitutes the framework for democratic debate of unprecedented magnitude. Never before have so many been able to relate so actively to so many political questions as is the case with the Net today. This has prompted many to acclaim deliberative democracy as a perspective for the development, i.e. a version of democracy in which ongoing discourse, arguments and debate between people and authorities ought to result in optimal political decisions, both in terms of legitimacy and content (Wilhelm 2000, p. 32ff). A network dynamic such as this ought to make it possible for everyone - including young people – to assert themselves. All else equal, it also ought to lead to greater participation.

d. The Internet opens up new forms of political participation. The Internet makes it possible for many to simultaneously act collectively, e.g. by sending emails to authorities with protests, requests, etc. It is also possible to contact the authorities and raise questions or demands in connection with a given case. Finally, it is also possible to participate in political arrangements, e.g. petitions and Internet-based meetings in which there are presentations, debate, etc. – just as in meetings in a village hall (Wilhelm 200, p. 105ff).

As such the Internet makes increased interest in politics and political participation possible, just as it opens up for new possibilities in terms of mobilisation, information, deliberation and participation. It is therefore entirely natural that many regard the Internet as having the potential to mobilise increased political involvement, particularly among those segments of the population that actively utilise the Internet today, not the least of whom are young people. However, the idea is also that the Internet generally ought to be able to have a mobilising effect on all groups who are now passive spectators or simply absent from the political public sphere. This is the case with senior citizens, members of society with few resources, those with little or no education and particularly young people. One can formulate this as a fundamental thesis, i.e. that the Internet, by virtue of its nature, has a stimulating effect on interest in politics and participation.

Studies have indicated that something happens with senior citizens when they get on the net, namely, once they have overcome their initial nerves and difficulties they are not entirely hopeless (Castells 2001, p. 119 ff.). This is less pronounced in the case of those with little or no education. Conversely, there is little to indicate that young people live up to expectations, even though there are no practical barriers to be overcome in connection with the Net. This relationship requires further illumination, but young people have yet to make a significant return to the political sphere as a result of dynamic use of the Internet.

VIRTUAL REALITY

One must begin by examining the Internet as a phenomenon before being able to deal more closely with the relationships between young people, the Internet and politics. One can pay notice to various aspects, e.g. the rapid dissemination of information and its accessibility (Dahlgren 2001). This is the traditional approach, which might be good enough. However, in this context it is far more fruitful to examine *the virtual reality* that the Net serves as the framework for. It is precisely by functioning as a medium establishing connection between a public and an expression that the Internet contributes to the moulding of a very particular reality, i.e. 'the reality of the Net', which it is necessary to relate to (Virilio 1998).

The Internet transmits diverse expressions to its public. The interactive expressions can consist of some semblance of community between a number of individuals, who at any given point in time communicate with one another about school, music, clothing, sex or something entirely different. When one meets a specific expression, the only reference one has is often to the Net itself, i.e. as an active participant in the community, one can present oneself as anyone, while nobody can check whether or not this is correct.

Not that this is terribly important – when a person moves out onto the Net, they engage in an agreement with a given sender that as long as they are together on the Net, they accept one another at face value – or else the one simply drops the other. In other words, one can be a lascivious 16-year-old young man or an experienced girl of 17 on the Net, while in another reality one might actually be a lonely 42-year-old man or a shy 12-year-old girl. The Net provides opportunity to live out a little dream about something else. It is somewhat inconsequential, however, for as long as one is on the Net; it is the reality of the Net that matters. This is the fundamental principle inherent to virtual reality, which can assume an infinite number of forms (Darley 2000, p. 184).

Unique rules of play are developed in these virtual contexts. One is who one says one is when moving out onto the Net. It is a context in which one's off-Net persona is of little consequence – if any at all. One is therefore only taken seriously on the Net. On the Net one is allowed to be brazen, vulgar, provocative, inquisitive, callous, coarse, brutal, or whatever happens to appeal to one on any given day; and the same applies to everybody else. It is not necessary to obey the normal rules governing interaction between people. One must merely follow the rules of the Net, the primary idea of which being to stimulate one another in the exciting projects that you engage in on the Net. The abrupt conclusion and choice of new contexts is entirely accepted as the next step in any virtual relationship. In short, relationships in virtual reality are regulated to a greater extent by excitement and stimulation than morals.

Of course there are some people who overstep these boundaries at regular intervals, i.e. where someone engages in actual contact with the person who has sent the stimulating information or expressions, risking pleasant surprise or terrible disappointment. In the meantime, this is rarely the central aspect of the virtual communication. To the contrary, it is the virtual reality that people construct together, facilitating new and stimulating experiences.

At the same time, the digital expressions achieve increasing impact by virtue of developments in digital technology, which seem to make almost everything possible. One can make digital, i.e. "living" representations of new spaces, houses, landscapes and social groups. One can produce new realities and spaces, new countries or whatever. There is talk of a graphic technology that supports the ability of the Net to disseminate the virtual reality. Moreover, this is not merely the case with the Net, but also on television, where digital technology is utilised, e.g. the reconstruction of central events by the news media (Darley 2000, p. 102ff). Combined with the Net, digital technology ensures immense potential for interactivity. The users themselves are able to repeatedly create their own image on the screen. The array of interactive computer games in which one plays with and against one another on the Net exemplify the expression of this virtual reality; a context in which one can ascertain that some features become increasingly apparent. The virtual (gaming) reality is marked by interaction and simulation. The central aspect in the computer game is not the narrative but rather the circumstance that one is active, i.e. that one is an active participant in a game in which one is capable of controlling events that are occurring in the present (Darley 2000, p. 157). One is not passive; one is active, here and now. There is no use for the capacity to tell stories or to reflect in abstract terms about past, present and future. There is a need for the capacity to act in relation to the given present, which can only be achieved by incessantly uncovering new and unknown threats and dark holes. This is how one plays up to fantasy and the powers of the imagination, as opposed to drawing on classical myths and rituals, which at the same time can also be present in a given game.

In a computer game, one experiences an image of an actual event in which new challenges are continuously encountered. The other players act in the present in a space characterised by the representation of imagery. The objective is to attain control over events, which in the meantime merely lead one to a higher level; which simply makes it even more exciting (Darley 2000, p. 162ff).

Based on this example, it is possible to make further observations pertaining to the role one assumes as an active user on the Net. The active Net user is not a *reader* and in that sense not an interpreter, either. The concerned individual is not looking to acquire a new story or narrative; rather, he is after action. The Net user is a *sensualist*, pursuing experiences and opportunities to play along (Darley 200, p. 169ff). In other words, neither the reflexivity nor powers of abstraction of the users of the Net are developed; rather, it is about the capacity to experience. The future of the Net will therefore involve the development of programming that facilitates greater sensation.

There is talk of a highly individualistic and occasionally also very egoistic role, playing up to a sensual dimension. This is first and foremost within oneself. One is also very private; Net activities often proceed within private and local spaces – while one is simultaneously coupled to the global Net (Darley 2000, p. 184). Many are indisputably empowered in front of the screen by virtue of the circumstance that they learn to deal with increasing aspects of the virtual reality and thereby also the virtual politics, for example, that it represents on the Net. At the same time, however, dependencies develop; just as simple as it is to deal with the virtual experiences of the Net, so can it be difficult to handle the normal routines in an everyday in which one must arm oneself with patience and the strength of reflexivity. Stated in brief, the empowerment of the Net user is Net-based and not immediately convertible – if at all – to another reality (Darley 2000, p. 174).

In other words, the digital reality fosters the development of an individual who first and foremost pursues stimulation and sensuality – as opposed to narratives and abstraction. The Net user can only realise this by being active, by attempting to control all situations and constantly playing in the present. While it is possible to find many other players, they are fleeting, primarily characterised by a common interest in Net activities.

The virtual reality facilitates the assumption of diverse roles in *real time*. One can act in a number of contexts. At the same time, the Net does not require courtesy. It is possible to fully experience the rules of the computer game, i.e. shoot first or risk defeat. This is the case in many contexts. Daily spam-mails are a good example of how the Net opens up for this lack of moral standards in intercourse with other computers. The same is the case with various worms and viruses that are constantly sent in circulation on the Net. These are all primarily the result of groups (of young people in particular) that discover new playing rules and spaces for their desire to play along on the Net in some game or another; e.g. hackers, worm-spreaders and the like. Eighteen-year-old Jeffrey Lee Parson, who was responsible for the Blaster virus in the summer of 2003, is an example of this phenomenon.

YOUNG PEOPLE ON THE NET

The familiarity of contemporary youth with the Net is beyond all doubt. For one thing, the Net is a part of normal teaching in schools and for another, it is the source of much of the daily input that plays a role in creating or confirming identities among young people, e.g. information about rock stars, film idols and other figures of interest. Many young people have experience with the creation of their own websites, just as they also spend much time communicating (Sørensen *et al.* 2002); a function that is not fulfilled by the Net alone, naturally, but it plays a central role in this regard. Table 1 presents calculations in terms of the frequency of the various generations' general use of the Internet, as well as the frequency of their use of the Internet in connection with acquiring information about politics and society.

Table 1. Frequency of use of the Internet, accounting for gender and age

Year	How often do you use the Internet?				How often do you use the Internet to find information about politics and society			
	Every day	Once a week or more	Less than once a week	Never	Every day	Once a week or more	Less than once a week	Never
Men								
1975-85	69	13	16	3	6	20	28	47
1960-74	65	16	7	12	9	15	32	44
1945-59	49	13	11	27	10	13	22	56
1930-44	18	28	8	46	0	8	8	85
before 1930	13	9	9	68	4	4	5	87
Women								
1975-85	39	44	9	8	2	23	38	38
1960-74	53	24	11	12	4	20	21	46
1945-59	39	21	16	25	5	10	22	63
1930-44	34	25	6	34	3	13	13	72
before 1930	8	3	5	84	2	1	3	94
total	42	18	10	30	5	13	22	60

Data: The Danish Democracy and Power Study, 2003. n: 988

The table illustrates that young people have a very familiar relationship to the Net. Almost 70 percent of young men use the Net on a daily basis, while young women are not quite as active. The table also shows that use of the Internet is inversely proportionate to age – the older you are, the less you use it. The lowest use of the net is found among elderly women, which is hardly surprising. In terms of using the Net in connection with acquiring information about politics and society, it is clear that segments of the '68-generation are the most active on an everyday basis. Generally, however, the number of persons pursuing this type of information via the Net is quite limited. Remarkably enough, young girls are generally slightly more active in terms of finding this type of information than young men. By and large, the information indicates that young men are very active on the Net, but this is largely in contexts that have little to do with politics and society. This is further confirmed by Table 2, which shows the Net activities of the various generations.

The table indicates that when it comes to following discussions about politics and society, as well as participating oneself in these discussions, it is the young men who are the most active beyond compare. The table also shows that there is not always particularly great distance from being a spectator to becoming active. For young men and women alike, there is no particular difference between following debates and oneself signing petitions. Conversely, the women have a slightly harder time plunging into the established chats and debates, which is also the case for the population on the whole. This emphasises two relationships: first, young people are familiar with the opportunities inherent to the Internet. Second, they have no difficulty resorting to action as long as they find themselves on the Net. However, the table also indicates with great clarity that young people particularly use the Net for activities that do not have anything to do with politics and society. It is primarily about acquiring information about music, films, sex, personal relationships, problems pertaining to youth, etc. – and engaging in discussions of the same (Stald 2001). The Net is also used for daily communication with friends, e.g. emails and SMS-messages sent via the Net and to be received and read on cell phones. Others meet in various chat contexts in which one also meets many strangers, but naturally the latter can also play along by virtue of assuming a given virtual role, e.g. by

Table 2. Use of the Internet, accounting for gender and age within the last 12 months t

Year born	Follow debates or chats about politics and society	Sign a peti- tion	Participate in debates or chats about politics and society	Follow de- bates or chats about subjects other than politics and society	Participate in debates or chats about subjects other than politics and society
Men					
1975-85	17	18	9	42	30
1960-74	10	16	5	26	7
1945-59	7	5	4	15	7
1930-44	3	0	3	10	3
before 1930	1	0	0	5	5
Women					
1975-85	9	17	2	29	9
1960-74	7	11	1	17	5
1945-59	6	10	1	9	4
1930-44	0	3	0	3	0
before 1930	0	0	0	0	0
Total	7	9	2	16	7

Data: The Danish Democracy and Power Study, 2003. n: 988

simply becoming active in a given dialogue about any kind of subject via the Net.

The Net is often also used for gaming, whether there is talk of card playing, adventure games, strategy games, battle games or something entirely different. There is a vast array of "game halls" on the Net, where one can have one's desires steered in this direction for free or at a very low price.

Finally, the Net is also used to embark upon voyages of discovery. Young people are proficient at *surfing* on the Net, because they are familiar with the opportunities available and they know exactly how to find the best websites. This ability can naturally be utilised in connection with attending to educational tasks, but the entertainment dimension is pursued to a slightly greater degree (Tapscott 1999).

The point is that as Net users, young people specifically pursue that which entertains and stimulates. Their sensual interests for exciting experiences, here and now first and foremost mark their behaviour on the Net. They pursue that which is exciting, entertaining and *emotionally* challenging. And it has to be in *real time*.

In this manner, the use of the Internet and computer games is registered in the contemporary youth culture in an entirely logical way. Today's young people are growing up in a world in which the making of decisions is that which is of central importance. They are raised to do so and the institutional contexts in which they live are also structured accordingly. Further to this point, young people can achieve security in two ways: either via education or consumption, which many of them then attempt to achieve. There are also groups of youth who choose other paths, e.g. autonomy. This can either be as an autonomous 'chaos pilot', busy making a difference in the contexts in which they happen to find themselves – preferably a difference that catches the attention of their surroundings. Alternatively they pursue the autonomy to be found in undeclared or 'black' work, cars that can burn tires and small pockets of local resistance, where the street corner still holds a great deal of meaning (Andersen 2001).

All of these young people have reflexivity as a fundamental condition of existence (Giddens 1996). In other words, they learn to manoeuvre in a world marked by choices in which they must make decisions, decisions that come to reflect upon their own identity. In brief, these choices are to be substantiated on their own basis, i.e. that young people are constantly moving about in contexts dominated by words and abstractions. They must regularly experience another reality, that being the physical sphere. In other words, contemporary youth culture is stretched out between two poles – head and body. The body is cultivated in many contexts, e.g. the annual Roskilde Festival just outside of Copenhagen, which is a kind of process of formation for young people, at normal parties, where intense drinking can also be a key to intense bodily experiences, in sport, dance, etc. (Andersen 2001).

Considered in this perspective, the computer culture suddenly seems far more understandable, as it precisely registers itself within the contemporary culture of youth in the central polarisation between head and body. The Internet and computer games are opportunities for a more sensuous and bodily reality. While it proceeds in isolation from the surrounding world and with one's nose planted directly in the screen, its emotional dimension is stimulating. One experiences the one 'kick' after the other when things are really grooving. On the face of things, one could be led to think that the comprehensive use of the Internet and computers by young people is owing to their reflexive culture and their ability to make independent decisions; a condition which naturally also has a certain amount of meaning. However, first and foremost it is the emotional aspect of the case that really counts. This is the reason that the behaviour of many youth in relation to the computer and the Net is as it is. They are frequent users in many contexts because they seek affirmation in terms of their identity, e.g. with the help of multitudes of SMS messages and because they are seeking a bodily experience – with the extra dimension that both parts are preferably to occur here and now.

THE POLITICS OF THE NET – NARRATIVE OR EXPERIENCE?

Long ago, Internet providers accepted the consequences of the circumstance that it is particularly the sensual and emotional dimensions of the users that are in focus when they go on the Net. The Internet is characterised to a diminishing extent by long texts and to an increasing extent by pictures and interactivity, the central point being that one has the opportunity to be active in connection with the image one has captured on the screen. Naturally there are still texts on the screen, but those that are placed in the upper levels of the Net are becoming shorter and shorter; also in primarily text-based contexts, such as information from authorities to citizens. And of course – also when it comes to politics.

This often results in inner opposition among the Internet providers with a textual basis who perceive opportunities to reach a greater audience via the Net, e.g. with public authorities and political organisations. They maintain a relatively large quantity of text, but at the same time they are aware that in the absence of exciting elements on a given website it is not possible to maintain the interest of very many others than those who are the most focused, interested and specialised users of the Net.

It is thus characteristic that among most of the providers it is becoming increasingly easy to orient oneself among their stories via pictures, while longer texts with greater perspectives and horizons disappear. It is also characteristic that an increasing number of gimmicks appear on the various websites, e.g. in September 2003, the Danish Social Democratic Party had an offer entitled: *What is your dream for the future?* If one clicked on the appropriate icon, one had the opportunity to send one's dreams, see the dreams of the Social Democrats and test oneself; altogether in something resembling an interactive game. In a thought-provoking manner, a little note was added to the test: *Remember, it's only for fun!* This captures the very logic. If there was not any fun to be had, then it would not be worth sticking around on the Social Democrats' website. And if it is not fun enough, one just wanders off, e.g. to the website of the Danish Liberal Party, where one can test one's knowledge in an interactive quiz at the same time as one sees the Prime Minister at a motor race in Jutland. And if that is not fun enough, one can proceed to a particular section especially designed for young people (*v-files.unge.nu*), which present different forms of interactivity. Should all of that not be enough, one can possibly choose yet another party (there are eight parties represented in the Danish parliament!), e.g. the website of the Socialist Peoples' Party, which provides the opportunity to send a postcard, or the Danish People's Party, where one can see films. Alternatively one can also choose something that to a far greater extent is geared to functioning in relation to the expectations of the young Net users.

The point is that the political sphere is based on narratives, abstractions, arguments and continuity – all of which is very poorly compatible with the format and logic of the Internet. It is based on interactivity and rapid impact, i.e. a logic emphasising instantaneous, concrete, and spontaneous expressions – and sudden shifts. In other words this is the complete opposite of the political sphere (Virilio 1998, p. 27). Attempts are made at reconciling the two spheres at regular intervals, which very quickly results in players in the political sphere taking risks in which they can come to appear quite ridiculous. It is for this reason that one often feels the need to make excuses or express reservations for that, which is presented on the Net, as in the aforementioned case with the Social Democrats. This merely reflects the fundamental opposition existing on the Internet between the logical and consecutive structure of politics and the interactive, spontaneous and incoherent structure of the Net (Dahlgren 2001, p. 52). As the development has shown thus far, there are clear tendencies towards the victory of the structure of the Internet, as it increasingly appears to mark the political structure, also among the political parties themselves.

YOUNG PEOPLE, THE INTERNET AND POLITICS

Politics deals with society, i.e. about ensuring fundamental conditions in society and developing others. The optimal framework for politics is democracy. The youth of today have developed a political culture characterised by limited interest in politics, but considerable interest in society, particularly in terms of their own placement in relation to society. This is an interest that they can fulfil via the Net, which provides them with the opportunity to cultivate the personal relations and interests, find dynamic experiences and achieve a certain measure of simulation of their own emotions. This is owing to the circumstance that the logic of the Internet is a spontaneous and emotional logic – as opposed to the logic of the narrative, abstraction or debate. The reality of the Internet is virtual and based on *real time* role-playing. This is in opposition to the reality of politics, which is often a reality of the future and always based on references to the past and present. It presupposes abstraction and long lines, perspectives. The result is that it can be somewhat difficult to separate the numerous optimistic conceptions that are often advanced concerning the Internet, politics and political participation.

Given that background, it is interesting to return to the introductory assumptions pertaining to the political and democratic potential of the Internet. The former touches upon the capacity of the Internet for mobilisation. As is apparent in my examination, there is evidence that many young people have genuinely been mobilised, e.g. signing petitions; however, this mobilisation has not made a difference in terms of the fact that the primary interest of young people still lies very far from the political sphere. Moreover, if the approach of young men to political activities on the Net is ground in hopes that they can experience some kind of a 'good time', then this form of political participation has a spontaneous character which brings to mind something resembling role-playing or the like, i.e. one signs a petition to see what happens, possibly even signing someone else's name. This cannot be checked. One plays a role. One plays along in politics and one plays along in the real Internet game. The difference between the two might not be so great, when it comes down to it. So while the Internet might well be able to mobilise political participation, it presumably first and foremost proceeds according to the conditions of virtual reality.

The next assumption deals with access to information. Also in this instance, one can begin by making clear that certain positive tendencies can indeed be traced. Many young people have been on the Net for the purpose of finding information about politics and society, particularly in connection with schoolwork. On the other hand, it is also clear that they do not exaggerate this aspect of the Net. Furthermore, they will inevitably run into the opposition associated with the combination of the Internet and politics, i.e. the young pursue spontaneous and 'cool' things, which the parties increasingly play into. This limits the amount of information about politics that young people actually get a hold of. They pursue the political sphere, but they do so according to the logic of the Internet. They view images, opportunities for interaction and brief statements, while the narratives and grand perspectives that are otherwise intrinsic to politics do not have a chance of getting through to them.

The third assumption deals with deliberation and democratic debate. The Net offers optimal opportunity for dialogue, opportunity which some young people do indeed make use of. However, their number does not correspond to the number of young people that are active in other forms of dialogue, e.g. chats about love, sex, music, films and other crucial issues. When one considers the logic of virtual reality in this context, it does not fortify one's faith in the prospects of deliberation. The capacity of young people to play roles, to challenge others and push everything to extremes – e.g. by killing everyone else in a game – can easily come to mean that also in this instance, the young are merely playing roles in the democratic debate, if they participate in it at all. The concern is that they merely assume the positions that they think will provide the most amusing results here and now – not in society, but in the debate. There have been hints of this in the websites of various football clubs, where fans 'puff themselves up' in loud, aggressive tones – on the Net, in any case. Many young people presumably are quite indifferent towards the moral demands that one makes in a democratic debate to the personal involvement and responsibility of one's opponent, as long as they – logically enough – also regard this aspect of the Internet as a game. For they have not experienced it to be anything else. Particularly as it is incredibly rare that democratic debates conducted on the Net have ever led to anything that the young people have ever heard of (Kaare Nielsen 2002, p. 31). Add to this the privatisation and autonomisation that is also a consequence of the digital logic (Hoff 2002, p. 51f).

Finally, there are expectations of increased political participation solely on the basis of the circumstance that a significant portion of this new activity can proceed via the Internet. On the face of it, this also looks promising. There are relatively many young people who have signed petitions, and Net-based petitions have become a more widespread activity among young people than traditional petitions on paper (Goul Andersen *et al.* 2001). However, once again the question becomes whether this activity is capable of overcoming the limitations inherent to the virtual political reality. There is little evidence indicating this to be the case. Some theoreticians have written that this situation opens up for a society in which all opposition (antagonisms) has the opportunity to unfold without interests or outside of the constricting framework of the public, resulting in a more direct political sphere, here and now (Dean 2002, p. 16ff). However, that which is to actually constitute these many antagonisms, aside from the logic of computer games – where the objective is generally to obliterate everyone else – is difficult to get a sense of. In that sense, this context is also lacking evidence indicating that it contributes to young people growing closer to the political and democratic norms.

It is precisely because the Internet is the framework for a virtual political reality that there is danger that the fundamental democratic norms become relaxed. One can venture out onto the Net and construct any fictitious persona – a character who happens to perfectly match a given campaign in terms of firing it up, such that the entertainment value is increased at any give point in time. For in the absence of fascination and entertainment, there is no motivation to hang around. This corresponds to patterns of action in many Internet games: one assumes a role and gives it everything one has, until one does not feel like doing so any longer. At which time it is possible to shift to a new, more exciting role.

Naturally this perspective does not become different merely because the context is political, unless one is mobilised in a different manner and genuinely wish to do something for a given case; also on the Net. However, the Net is then no longer the central media capable of mobilising something extra. Then it is merely a channel for the communication of a sense of involvement that is chosen in other contexts.

Also in relation to politics, young people on the Net will play roles and they will pursue that which stimulates them. The moral foundation of the democratic involvement is thereby undermined. People are merely saying things, playing along, and making demands – without considering how they are to be held accountable for these statements and demonstrations. One is never held personally accountable on the Net. The only thing to be held accountable is the role that one assumed, a role that is merely *virtual*.

In this contribution I have attempted to encircle some of the dynamics that come into play in the interaction between young people, the Internet and politics. Many will likely say that the result is a tale of decay. My response to such critique would be that I have merely attempted to pursue a specific logic and a specific perspective. Had one chosen to pursue others, then perhaps they would have led to other – more optimistic – observations. However, that would be of no consequence to the bottom line: young people have not become more interested in politics since the emergence of the Internet, nor has their participation in politics increased.

REFERENCES

Andersen, J (2001) *Mellem hoved og krop. Om ungdomskulturer.* Århus Systime.

Andersen, J. (2003) "Uddannelse til demokrati - alle pædagogers drøm." in *KRAKA* nr. 22, August.

Castells, M. (2001) *The Internet Galaxy. Reflections on the Internet, Business and Society.* Oxford University Press, Oxford.

Dahlgren, P (2001) "The public Sphere and the Net: Structure, Space and Communication" in W. Lance Bennet, et al. (ed.). *Mediated Politics. Communication in the Future of Democracy*. Cambridge University Press. Cambridge.

Darley, A. (2000) "Visual digital culture. Surface play and spectacle" *in new media Genres*. Routledge, London.

Dean, J. (2002) "Kommunikativ kapitalisme: hvorfor nettet ikke er den offentlige sfære", in *GRUS* nr. 67.

Giddens, A. (1996) *Modernitet og selvidentitet. Selvet og samfundet under sen-moderniteten*. Hans Reizels Forlag. København.

Gimmler, A. (2001) "Deliberative democracy, the public sphere and the Internet", in *Philosophy & Social Criticism*. Sage.

Goul Andersen, J., L. Torpe & J. Andersen. (2000) *Hvad folket magter. Demokrati, magt og afmagt*. Djøf forlaget, København.

Hoff, J. (2002) "Demokratiforestillinger og magt i informationssamfundet," in *GRUS* nr. 66.

Kaare Nielsen, H. (2002) "De nye medier, kulturen og demokratiet", in *GRUS* nr. 66.

Levinsen, K. (2003) "Unge, individualisering og politik," in *KVAN* nr. 66.

Sparks, C. (2001) "The Internet and the Global Public Sphere", in W. Lance Bennet et al. (ed.). *Mediated Politics. Communication in the Future of Democracy*. Cambridge University Press. Cambridge.

Stald, G. (2001) "Ude er godt, hjemme er bedst", in *CEFU*, nr. 5, nettidsskrift RUC.

Sørensen, B. H., C. Jessen og B. R. Olesen. (2002) *Børn på nettet - kommunikation og læring*. Gads forlag, København.

Tapscott, D. (1999) *Growing Up Digital: The Rise of the Net Generation*. McGraw-Hill Education, New York 1999

Virilio, P. (1998) *Cyberworld - det værstes politik*. Introite! København.

Wilhelm A.G. (2000) *Democracy in the Digital Age. Challenges to Political Life in Cyberspace*. Routledge. New York.

CHAPTER 8

Adoption, Usage, and Impact of the Internet
Youth Participation and the Digital Divide in China

BU WEI

YOUTH ADOPTION OF THE INTERNET IN CHINA

As is well known, the population of children and youth in China is huge. According to China Statistical Bureau, it is estimated that about 29 per cent of the population are youngsters under 19, and numbered more than 369 million in 2002.[1] Among them, some have had access to the Internet since 1995. The survey reports from CNNIC (China Internet Network Information Centre) show that the numbers of youth users have increased as adult users have been expanding swiftly in China. The data of CNNIC is showed as Table 1. Up to July 2003, 17.1 per cent of users population is youngsters

More and more Chinese teenagers especially those who live in urban areas have been exposed to the technology of the new media since 1990. According to a national survey on media usage for 10-15 year olds in urban areas, 13.2 per cent of children had experience with computers in 1992[2]. The survey in 1996 of 14 major cities showed that 20.6 per cent of households

---

1. This data is accounted according to China Statistical Bureau, 2002 population by age and sex, China Population Statistics Yearbook 2002. The total population was 1,258,951,000 and youngersters under 19 is 369,268,000.

2. Bu Wei, "Entering into the Globe Village –Mass Communication and Chinese Children, Sichuang Chilldren" Publishing House, 1996, p.75.

Table 1 Statistics on youth users (Unit: 10 thousand)

	Total Users	Under 16	16-20	Under 18
Oct 1997	62	0.3 %	5.3%	
Jul 1998	117.5	4.0%	7.9%	
Jan 1999	210	0.7%	9.4%	
Jul 1999	400	0.7%	9.8%	
Jan 2000	890			2.4%
Jul 2000	1690			1.65%
Jan 2001	2250			14.93%
Jul 2001	2650			15.1%
Jan 2002	3370			15.3%
Jul 2002	4580			16.3%
Jan 2003	5910			17.6%
Jul 2003	6800			17.1%

Source CNNIC survey reports, www.cnnic.net.cn, September 7, 2003

with 10 –15-year-old children owned computers.[3] Up till 1998, five cities - including Beijing, Shanghai, Guangzhou, Zhengzhou and Chengdu - had 22.9 per cent of teenagers (aged 10-15) with computers in their home and 2.6 per cent of these computers had connections to the Internet.[4] In the same year in Beijing, 42.4 per cent of teenagers (aged 10-18) had computers at their home, and 8.4 per cent of these computers were connected to the Internet. Another 20 per cent of teenagers surfed the Web and chatted online in Cyber cafes or other places with Internet access.[5].

---

3.   Bu Wei, The influence of Mass Media on Children in China, 2001, Xinhua Publishing House, p.99.

4.   Bu Wei, The influence of Mass Media on Children in China, 2001, Xinhua Publishing House, p.101.

5.   Bu Wei, The influence of Mass Media on Children in China, 2001, Xinhua Publishing House, p.103.

Besides using computers or the Internet in families, urban youth have some chances to use this new media technology in their schools. Up till September 2001, 92.15 per cent of high schools and 65.32 per cent of middle schools in big or middle sized cities gave a course on information technology. The proportion is estimated to be 10.33 per cent for urban elementary schools; as at the end of 2001, there were 3.670 million computers in high, middle and elementary schools. That means that on average there are 51 students per computer. Also 10687 schools established a school intranet. These comprised 1.8 per cent of all national high, middle and elementary schools, and represented an increase of 3.56 since 1999[6]. According to a Beijing urban youth survey in 1998, 76 per cent of youth and children were able to learn computers in their schools, and 14.2 per cent of youth had joined computer groups[7].

Most youth began to have access to the Internet in 1999 and 2000. The survey report on youth and the Internet showed that 37.7 per cent of youth in Beijing, Shanghai, Guangzhou, Chengdu and Changsha use the Internet, and about 80 per cent of users began to use it during 1999 or 2000[8].

YOUTH USE OF THE INTERNET AND THEIR PARTICIPATION

In theinformation age, ICT (Information communication technology) is usually regarded as being one of the important tools of e-governance or e-democracy. E-governance is the public sector's use of information and communication technologies with the aim of improving information and service delivery, encouraging citizen participation in the decision-making

---

6. Chen Zhili, Development and Expectation on Using Information Technology into Education, China Information Almanac2002, 2002, China Information Almanac Publishing House, p.2.

7. Bu Wei, The influence of Mass Media on Children in China, 2001, Xinhua Publishing House, p.103.

8. Bu Wei and Guo Liang, Survey on the Internet Usage and impact among Teenagers in Beijing, Shanghai, Guangzhou, Chengdu and Changsha in 2000, China Informaiton Almanac2002, 2002, China Information Almanac Publishing House, p.969.

process and making government more accountable, transparent and effective[9]. Because the idea of adopting ICTs is to move beyond passive information-giving to active citizen involvement in the decision-making process, participation in society has become "a key cornerstone of good governance"[10].

In today's world, participation by children and youth is widely based on the UN Convention on the Rights of the Child. So far 192 countries, including China, have signed this UN Convention. Besides promoting the basic rights to life, security and development for children, the UN Convention also regulates a series of articles on the rights of child participation in society. Its core is presented in article 12 whereby the child has "the right to express those views freely in all matters affecting the child". Accordingly, in the Convention state authorities must ensure that children can exercise their rights to access the media and information, to freedom of expression, to freedom of thought, conscience and religion, to freedom of association and peaceful assembly, and to participation in cultural and artistic activities.[11] How can youth participate in society and have an impact on the process of decision-making? These articles are very related to information access and expression. Here, we see the possibilities to youth participation in society through the Internet because of the strong interaction function of the Internet.

Actually, some social experiments about promoting youth participation through the Internet have developed, such as UNESCO's "Infoyouth" project, which provided youth with media literacy training, developed youth information networks or NGOs, and established cyber café's or computer centers in the Congo, Afghanistan, India, Finland and other countries, so that youth can obtain the opportituties, abilities and experience for social participation[12].

Getting access to the Internet seemed an opportunity for e-governance and then democratization. But some scholars have challenged this common

---

9.   OECD, 2001, http://portal.unesco.org/ci/, December 12, 2003.

10.   OECD, 2001, http://portal.unesco.org/ci/, November 1, 2003.

11.   See the UN Convention on the Rights of the Child, 12?13,14,15,17,23,29,31 articles?

12.   UNISCO, http://portal.unesco.org/ci/

hypothesis. One of challenges is "the incredible inequity in terms of access to information technologies" [13]. Indeed, "E-government can make government institutions more transparent, help citizens to obtain access to public information and broaden their participation in the democratic processes. But it is doubtful that all these possibilities can be fully realized today or in the every near future, because only a small proportion of the world population has access to the Internet" [14]. In China, only 4-6 per cent of the population has access to the Internet, and much of the current users base comprises privileged young students 30.1 per cent and intellectuals 15.9 per cent. Young users under 30 account for 73.4 per cent of total users in China in 2002[15]. It is very difficult to see that the Internet can enhance political opportunities for all classes in all geographic regions, among both urban and rural populations, in the near future. Although the Internet may provide a new medium for dissent and opposition, its impact is offset by two principal factors – the digital divide and growing commercialization[16]. In particular, given the stark inequalities in terms of race, gender, education and income, Internet activism is predominantly an elite pastime[17]. In short, the technology itself may neither change society nor create democracy automatically.

In our study on youth and social participation in China, Firstly, we noticed that some youth did not have access to the Internet in urban areas.

---

13. Randy Kluver and Jack Linchuan Qiu, China, the Internet and Democracy, Rhetoric and Reality: The Internet Challenge for Democracy in Asia, Nanyang Technological University, Eastern Universities Press, 2003, p.55

14. Irian Netchaeva, E-Government and E-Democracy: a Comparison of Opportunities in the North and South, The International Journal for Communication Studies, VOL 64(5): 467

15. CNNIC, Survey on users in China in 2002, www.cnnic.net.com, December 12, 2003.

16. Jason P. Abbott, Democracy@internet.asia? The challenges to the emancipatory potential of the net: lessons from China and Malaysia, Third World Quarterly, Vol 22, No 1, pp 99, 2001

17. Jason P. Abbott, Democracy@internet.asia? The challenges to the emancipatory potential of the net: lessons from China and Malaysia, Third World Quarterly, Vol 22, No 1, pp 111,2001?

As for rural areas, to find the relevant statistics on rural youth use of the Internet from Chinese statistical documents or reports. This means that most youth do not use the Internet. That is why that our research focus is on who is likely to be Internet users in China. Although the adoption of the Internet is not equal to the e-democracy, having access to the Internet would be the first step for equal participation. Secondly, we focus on the users use of the Internet such as: what do youth do online after they have access to the Internet? Is their usage related (or not) to their social participation? Is it possible that youth use of the Internet promotes their social participation?

RESEARCH DESIGN

Research questions

The study will focus on two issues. Firstly, so far, what kind of youth has adopted the Internet, or under which conditions is it easier for youth to access the Internet?

According to the 2000 Survey Report on Internet Usage and its impact among Teenagers in Beijing, Shanghai, Guangzhou, Chengdu and Changsha, youth adoption of the Internet was found to reflect significant differences in gender, age, parents' education background, parents' occupation, and family income[18]. This study will not use the diffusion of innovation theory[19] found in communication studies to explore youth adoption of the new technology. This is because (1) adoption of the Internet is still at its and initial stages in China, with many "hard" conditions such as family income, connectivity more important than "soft" conditions such as personal attitudes (i.e. very much related to the digital divide) (2) unlike adults, youth and children are much more likely to be influenced by their surroundings. It is observed that adoption by family (parents buy computer for their children) or schools' adoption (teachers giving a course on computers or the Internet

---

18.   Bu Wei and Guo Liang, Survey on the Internet Usage and it's impact among Teenagers in Beijing, Shanghai, Guangzhou, Chengdu and Changsha in 2000, China Informaiton Almanac2002, 2002, China Information Almanac Publishing House, p.971–973.

19.   Everett M. Rogers, *Diffusion of Innovations* (third edition),New York; The Free Press,1982; Forth edition, New York; The Free Press, 1995.

in school) can directly affect youth adoption of the Internet. Therefore, we explore the factors that affected youth adoption (conducting this research through individual interview, focus groups and fieldwork in cyber cafés or children homes) rather than these factors are framed by the diffusion of innovation theory. In this study, the following factors will be discussed: regional differences, family differences (parents' education background, parents occupation, income, support and adoption in family), school differences (adoption into education), and personal difference (gender and age).

Secondly, in international development, "participation is a process through which stakeholders influence and share control over development initiatives and the decisions and resources which affect them"[20]. As stakeholders, Chinese youth may have a participatory access to express their views via the Internet. On the basis of pilot study, we will test youth users' participation through the following indexes:

(1) Do you use forum or bulletin board systems?

(2) Which is the best avenue when you want to express your views about society or school?

(3) Do you like to express your views about society or school more or less since you began using the Internet?

We suppose that these three have a significant correlation.

As everybody knows, use of the Internet is not the same as social participation. This study will analyze the meanings of youth' participation by exploring users experiences and their motivations for Internet use. Moreover, the possibility of youth participation in society through the Internet will be discussed.

Method
This is an exploratory research because Chinese youth adoption of the Internet is at the initial stage now and very little evidence has been found or theories developed in the communication field. Accordingly, we started our research by conducting interviews. The aim was to develop research

---

20.   The Final Report of the Participation Learning Group within the World Bank, http://trochim.human.cornell.edu/gallery/katsumotshuzo.html#participation %20as, 26 December 2003.

content and structure by collecting data among youth. Initially, there were two individual in-depth interviews, three focus groups were queried and one questionnaire survey was conducted in Beijing. The researchers developed this questionnaire based on the interviews. Thereafter, a sampling survey was conducted in seven cities in China from February to April of 2003.

Sample

Since most Chinese Internet users live in large or medium-sized cities or urban areas, the survey was concentrated on the major cities including Beijing, Shanghai, Guangzhou, Chengdu, Changsha, Xining and Huhhot. The survey population covered students in elementary schools (10-12 years old), middle and high schools in these seven cities. The target populations in the study were; (1) students from the seven cities; and (2) students from above each city. The original sample (3400) was weighted according to the sizes of each subpopulation (number of students in each city). The weighted sample size was 3375.

Considering the unbalanced development of cities in China, we selected Beijing, Shanghai and Guangzhou as developed cities, Chengdu and Changsah as less developed cities, and Xining and Huhhot as developing cities according to the 2001–2002 China Cities Development Report[21]. This report ranked 50 cities in China by 104 indexes for development. Table 2.1 presented the rank for these seven cities by 4 synthetic indexes. We have added the number of users in these seven cities from CNNIC statistics for reference

The actual sampling error was estimated in this study by reference to two key variables: the proportion of Internet users and proportion of family computers.

Proportion of Internet users. While each city is respectively as a population and the confidence level is 90 per cent, the sampling error is respectively: Beijing, 5.9 per cent; Shanghai, 7.2 per cent; Guangzhou, 5.8 per cent; Chengdu, 8.5 per cent; Changsha, 5.1 per cent; Xining, 5.8 per cent; Huhhot, 8.9 per cent. While total seven cities are as a population and the confidence level is 90 per cent, the sampling error of adoption of the Internet is 3.2 per cent.

Proportion of family computers. While each city is respectively as a population and the confidence level is 90 per cent, the sampling error is

---

21. China Mayor Asscociation 2003 China Cities Development Report 2001–2002, Xiyuan Publishing House.

respectively: Beijing, 5.6 per cent; Shanghai, 5.0 per cent; Guangzhou, 5.2 per cent; Chengdu, 5.1 per cent; Changsha, 5.1 per cent; Xining, 6.5 per cent; Huhhot, 6.4 per cent. While total seven cities were taken as a population and the confidence level is 90 per cent, the sampling error of having the computers in households is 2.4 per cent.[22].

Table 2.1 Cities Development Level and the Number of Internet Users

City	Rank of city synthetic strength[a]	Rank of city development potential[b]	Rank of city development capability[c]	Rank of Information level[d]	Users % of population
Beijing	2	3	2	2	6.6%
Shanghai	1	2	1	1	7.1%
Guangzhou	3	4	4	4	Guangdong 9.5%
Chengdu	21	32	23	34	Sichuan 5.2%
Changsha	24	16	24	20	Hunan 2.9%
Huhhot	45	43	46	49	Huhhot 1.2%
Xining	49	48	49	45	Qinghai 0.3%

a.   The city synthetic strength is composed of 12 indexes, see China Mayor Association 2003, 2001 –2002 China Cities Development Report, Xiyuan Publishing House, p.296.

b.   The city developing potential is composed 104 indexes, see China Mayor Association 2003 2001 –2002 China Cities Development Report, Xiyuan Publishing House, p.298.

c.   The city development capacity come from weighting on "potential" by "strength", see China Mayor Association 2003, 2001–2002 China Cities Development Report, Xiyuan Publishing House, p.302.

d.   The information developing level is integrated by 5 indexes, see China Mayor Association 2003, 2001 –2002 China Cities Development Report, Xiyuan Publishing House, p.337.

MAIN FINDINGS

Youth adoption of the Internet

In the study, user is defined as teenage student who uses the Internet on average more than one minute per week[23]. Differences in regional school, family and person are taken as factors that affect youth adoption in these seven cities based on the hypothesis.

Regional differences in Internet adoption

The survey showed that the average proportion of Internet adoption in seven cities is 63.3 per cent (N=3375). As seen in table 3.11, an adoption rule greater than 60 per cent occurred in developed cities like Beijing, Shanghai, Guangzhou and less developed Changsha. A low proportion of adoption is found in developing Xining and Huhhot.

Table 3.11 Adoption of the Internet in seven cities

City	Bei-jing	Shang -hai	Guang -zhou	Cheng -du	Chang -sha	Xining	Huhhot
Percent	66.9	61.5	73.3	52.6	78.4	37.1	43.8
N	498	497	457	492	485	442	438

In the early days of the Internet adoption in China, this was closely related to computer ownership in households. The significant correlation is found between the adoption of the Internet and the computer ownership in households (P=.000). The significant variance of computer ownership between seven cities is also found (P=.000). Successively, they are: Guangzhou, 84.5 per cent; Beijing, 81.3 per cent; Changsha, 59.9 per cent; Shanghai, 58.7 per cent; Chengdu, 48.8 per cent; Xining, 36.9 per cent; Huhhot, 35.4 per cent.

Generally speaking, "using the Internet at home," means that users have a personal computer, telephone line and modem, also that users have

---

22.   Details see the Survey Report on Youth Adoption, Use, and Impacts of the Internet in Seven Cities in China, in April 2003.

23.   Some teenagers used the Internet very occasionally, and would like to answer the questionnaire, but these answers are much less confident. We discriminated and deleted these questionnaires during the survey and after the survey.

better economic conditions. In contrast, "using the Internet in Cyber café" means poorer conditions among youth users. The survey proved this point. As seen in Table 3.12, there is a significant variance of "using the Internet at home" between the seven cities (P=.000), likewise in Table 3.13, a significant variance in "using the Internet in "cyber cafe" can be seen.

Table 3.12 Regional difference in "using Internet at home" in per cent N=1870?

	Beijing	Shang-hai	Guang-zhou	Chengdu	Changsha	Xining	Huhhot
Never	10.0	28.2	8.5	39.1	38.8	45.9	49.1
Sometimes	16.9	11.7	8.2	15.0	12.2	14.9	11.7
Often	11.2	10.0	10.5	12.4	12.8	11.5	12.3
Very often	61.9	50.2	72.8	33.5	36.2	27.7	26.9
	100.0	100.0	100.0	100.0	100.0	100.0	100.0

Table 3.13, Regional difference in "using the Internet in "cyber cafes" in per cent N=1890

	Beijing	Shanghai	Guang-zhou	Chengdu	Changsha	Xining	Huhhot
Never	83.3	72.8	75.9	39.9	39.9	35.2	31.1
Sometimes	8.3	10.5	14.4	23.1	26.2	27.0	31.1
Often	4.0	6.6	5.7	18.5	20.8	16.4	11.5
Very often	4.3	10.1	4.0	18.5	13.1	21.4	26.2
	100.0	100.0	100.0	100.0	100.0	100.0	100.0

We can see that high proportions of "using the Internet at home" are found in Guangzhou (91.5 per cent), Beijing (90 per cent) and Shanghai (71.8 per cent); low rates (of about 50 per cent) are found in Xining and Huhhot; with Chengdu and Changsha in the middle, at about 60 per cent. In contrast, the percentage of "using Internet in a cyber café" is highest in Xining and Huhhot (68.9 per cent and 64.8 per cent). Lower in Chengdu and Changsha (about 60 per cent), and quite low in Guangzhou (24.1 per cent), Shanghai (27.2 per cent) and Beijing (16.7 per cent), the percentage of "using Internet in cyber café" is less low. This result indicated the significant variance between the developed, less developed and developing regions. Generally, users who have not Internet resources in their homes rely more on the public cyber cafes. The statistics proved this point (P=.000), as can be seen in table 3.14.

Table 3.14 Cross statistics between "having Internet resource" and "using Cyber café"
N=1963

	Having or having not Internet access at homes		
Using cyber cafés	No	Yes	Total
Never	51.9%	76.5%	69.3%
Sometimes/very often	48.1%	23.5%	30.7%
Total	100.0%	100.0%	100.0%

In addition, a statistical correlation between Internet access at home versus at cyber cafés showed that apart from Beijing and Guangzhou there were significant differences in the other 5 cities with a high degree of adoption when youth had more diverse choices (see Table 3.15)

School differences in Internet adoption

In China, there is access to the Internet in some schools. The survey revealed that more adopters are found in schools that have access to the Internet than in those schools that do not. There is a significant variance between "having access" and "having not access" (P=.000) in schools.

Especially, if schools adapt computers or the Internet for teaching, this brings about more adoptions. There are two pieces of evidence supporting this here. (1) More adopters used computer to finish their schoolwork. The significant variance is found between "using computer" and "not using computer" (P=.000); (2) more adopters used the Internet to finish their school works. Here again, the significant variance is found between "using the Internet" and "not using the Internet" (P=.000).

Table 3.15 Cross statistics on family Internet resource And using cyber café in seven cities

		Having or having not Internet access at home			Chi square Test P	N
	Whether or not using cyber café	No	Yes	Total		
Beijing	Never	86.3%	82.7%	83.3%	0.533	323
	From sometimes to very often	13.7%	17.3%	16.7%		
	Total	100.0%	100.0%	100.0%		
Shanghai	Never	60.4%	80.4%	73.0%	0.000	285
	From sometimes to very often	39.6%	19.6%	27.0%		
	Total	100.0%	100.0%	100.0%		
Guang-zhou	Never	70.0%	76.5%	75.5%	0.326	314
	From sometimes to very often	30.0%	23.5%	24.5%		
	Total	100.0%	100.0%	100.0%		
Chengdu	Never	24.8%	51.2%	39.2%	0.000	232
	Sometimes to very often	75.2%	48.8%	60.8%		
	Total	100.0%	100.0%	100.0%		
Changsha	Never	17.1%	59.8%	39.7%	0.000	348
	Sometimes to very often	82.9%	40.2%	60.3%		
	Total	100.0%	100.0%	100.0%		
Xining	Never	18.1%	54.7%	35.4%	0.000	158
	Sometimes to very often	81.9%	45.3%	64.6%		
	Total	100.0%	100.0%	100.0%		
Huhhot	Never	13.9%	51.8%	31.0%	0.000	184
	Sometimes to very often	86.1%	48.2%	69.0%		
	Total	100.0%	100.0%	100.0%		

We also found that school adoption is very much related to regional differences. More students in developed and less developed cities said that their school has access to the Internet, teachers asked them to finish their homework by computer, and teachers asked them to finish their homework using the Internet than those students in developing cities. This is shown as Table 3.2.

Table 3.2 Cities difference in school adoption (N=3370)

	Beijing	Shang -hai	Guang -zhou	Chengdu	Chang -sha	Xining	Huhhot	Chi- square
School access	49.7%	45.8%	55.2%	48.3%	51.5%	21.6%	17.6%	P=.000
Using computer	52.3%	39.4%	50.3%	27.6%	29.2%	14.3%	11.2%	P=.000
Using Internet	63.5%	45.5%	57.2%	43.1%	57.2%	23.1%	28.1%	P=.000

Family differences in Internet adoption

The study found that parents' education level, family income, popularity of the Internet among relatives or friends and support from parents are factors that affect youth adoption as follows:

(1) The user's father educational level is significantly higher than that of non-users (P=.000). The educational level of users' parents is significant (P=.000).

(2) Family income among users is significantly higher than for non-users (P=.000), (see Table 3.31). This doesn't mean that most families with Internet access have a good income, but it suggests that there is a higher proportion of users coming from higher-income families than non-users, and that there a lower proportion of users in lower income families than non-users.

(3) Internet adoption among users' relatives or friends is significantly higher than it is for non-users (P=.000). When asked whether most relatives or friends had adopted the Internet, about 50 per cent of users answered "yes"; among non-users this was only 22.6 per cent.

(4) There is a significant variance in parental support between users and non-users (P=.000). When asked, " do your parents support your adoption of the Internet", 79.2 per cent of users said "yes"; among non-users this was only 59.7 per cent.

Table 3.31 what is the average monthly income in your family? (N=2364)

	Non-users	Users
2000 Yuan and below	61.4%	36.1%
2001-4000 Yuan	27.4%	37.0%
4000 Yuan and above	11.2%	27.0%
Total	100.0%	100.0%

Individual differences in Internet adoption

The study revealed that more boys have adopted the Internet than girls. Male users comprised 67.4 per cent of total boys (N=1582), while female users comprised 59.3 per cent of total girls (N=1746). There was significant variance between the two genders P=.000

Another individual difference relates to age. The statistics showed that the older users are, the higher the adoption rates whereas 54.0 per cent students in elementary schools (N=1186) had adopted the Internet, this rate rose to 60.2 per cent among students in middle schools (N=1448) and 87.0 per cent students in high schools (N=662), while the significant variance is found between ages (P=.000), numerically most users are fond among students in middle schools because of their huge population.

We can see that Internet adoption has revealed significant regional differences. As in the digital divide found in other countries, more adopters are from developed and less developed cities. The regional difference is also found in the Internet adoption among schools, place of access (at home or in cyber cafés), whether or not the family is likely to have a computer and so on. In developed and less developed cities, more youth have personal computers, have adopted the Internet and use the Internet at their homes than is the case for those students from developing cities.

With regard to family influence on the Internet adoption, the main factors are parents' educational levels, family income, and popularity of the Internet among relatives or friends, as well as support from parents. The study proved that family income is a key factor because it has significant correlation with "education" (father's education: $R=.422$, $P=.000$, $N=2268$; mother's education: $R=.400$, $P=.000$, $N=2284$), "popularity" ($R=.256$, $P=.000$, $N=2175$) and "support" ($R=.160$, $P=.000$, $N=2386$). When in the survey, we asked non-users why they had not adopted the Internet, 44.2 per cent of respondents replied that there are not computers in their homes.

The individual difference is mainly represented in gender and age. More boys from high or middle schools have adopted the Internet. Apart from age, all the above-mentioned differences could be taken as evidence for a digital divide.

Youth use of the Internet and social participation
As mentioned above, 63.3 per cent of youth have adopted to the Internet in these seven cities. The statistics also showed that 72.5 per cent of users have less than three years' experience on the Internet; 51.2 per cent of users spend less 60 minutes weekly on the Internet; Most users use the Internet on Fridays, Saturdays and Sundays, and about 20 per cent of users spend three hours online during weekends. Between Monday and Thursday, users spend on average, 1-2 hours online per week. As such, what we want to know is what users do online and the relations between youth usage and social participation via the Internet.

Youth participation online
This study tested youth users' participation through following questions:

A. Do you use forum or BBS?

B. Which is the best avenue when you want to express your views about society or school?

C. Do you like to express your views about society or school more or less since you began using the Internet?

The significant correlation is found between A and B ($r=.169$, $p=.000$, $N=1995$), A and C ($r=.335$, $p=.000$, $N=1956$), and B and C ($r=.117$, $p=.000$, $N=1986$). The statistics showed that forums or expression or participation.

However, there are few grounds for optimism if we look at youth use of forum or BBS - 51.8 per cent of users "never" use forum or BBS and 30.4 per cent of users only "occasionally" use them. Only 13.1 per cent of users "often" and a mere 4.8 per cent of users "daily" use these services (N=2049), which have not become an all-pervading vehicle for youth expression or participation. Rather, 51 per cent of users might rather choose the Internet when needing to express their views about society, while 41 per cent of users' choice is television, and 42 per cent of users' choice is newspapers.

On the other hand, using the Internet encouraged users' self-expression and social participation. The statistics showed that 39.5 per cent of respondents said that they now liked to express views about society after they began using the Internet. Moreover, the more time users spend online, the more dependence they have on Internet as a means of expression. The statistics are as follows: 45 per cent of users, who spend 1.5 hours per weekly, have needs for expression by Internet; when users spend 1.5–3 hours, the proportion increases to 49 per cent; And when users spend 3–6 hours, the proportion rises to 64 per cent (p=.000, N=2014).

What do they do online?

Looking at forum or BBS in combination with other usages of the Internet, we can observe the importance and nature of forum or BBS for youth users. Of 14 online options, the users choose, on average, 7.2 different options. The most popular options are online surfing (54.4 per cent, N=2037) and playing games (48.3 per cent N=2062), followed by searching online (47.8 per cent, N=2047); downloading (47.6 per cent, N=2058); going into chat rooms (31.0 per cent, N=2058); using e-mail (22.2 per cent, N=2060); and OICQ (21.1 per cent, N=2054). Less popular options are Forum or BBS (17.9 per cent, N=2049); news subscriptions (16.7 per cent N=2065); developing web pages and sites (13.5 per cent, N=2041); uploading (12.8 per cent, N=2031); Internet telephony (8.2 per cent, N=2053); setting up proxy servers (7.4 per cent, N=2053); and online shopping (6.2 per cent, N=2055). It is obvious that forum or BBS is not very popular among youth users.

The correlation between forum/BBS and other usages of the Internet are examined through a factor analysis (Rotated Component Matrix). The factor analysis showed that three common factors could be extracted from the 14 Internet options, namely a technical factor (F1), a practical factor (F2), and an entertainment/communication factor (F3). The eigenvalue was >1, the loading value was >0.3 and cumulative rate was 53.15 per cent. Their variance was respectively 19.89 per cent, 19.00 per cent and 14.23 per cent.

F1 comprised proxy servers (.701); developing web pages (.684); subscribing to news (.673); online shopping (.663); using Internet telephony (.596); uploading (.478); using Forum or BBS (.366).

F2 comprised searching online (.816); downloading (.764); surfing (.676); using E-mail (.547); uploading (.448); and using Forum or BBS (.425).

F3 comprised using chat rooms (.753); playing games (.663); using OICQ (.619); using Forum or BBS (.520); and using Email (.303).

We can see that the loading value of "Forum or BBS" exceeds 0.3 for all three factors. The loading value is highest for the entertainment/communication factor, followed by the practical factor, the technical factor having the lowest score. However, it is important to note that when youth Use "Forum or BBS" it is not necessarily because they wish to be socially engaged as the usage is significantly related entertainment /communication as well as practical and technical interests.

CONCLUSION AND DISCUSSION

We can deduce three main conclusions from this study.

Firstly, we found that 63.3 per cent of youth in Beijing, Shanghai, Guangzhou, Chengdu, Changsha, Xining, and Huhhot have adopted the Internet. However we also found significant differences in terms of how regions, schools, families and individuals had adopted the Internet. Generally speaking, more youth have adopted the Internet in the more developed cities, in schools with greater access to the Internet, in families with higher income and better educational background. There is thus typical "digital divide" at the initial stage of Internet adoption.

A typical user could be described as a boy, who is a student in middle- or high school; who uses computers for homework and together with classmates; his family has good income enabling him to buy a personal computer and surf online at home; his parents have a good educational background, and have also adopted the Internet; the boy lives in Beijing or Guangzhou.

Secondly, most users didn't use the Internet for expressing their political views or participation in society when "using forum or BBS". 51.8 per cent of users "never" used forum or BBS; only 17.9 per cent often used "forum or BBS". It is thus clear that forum or BBS have not become an all-pervasive means for youth to express their ideas or participate in cyberspace forums. Besides, about 50 per cent of users didn't choose the Internet for expressing their views on society. However, this study did find that using the Internet encouraged users' to express their ideas or participate in political discussions.

Thirdly, compared to surfing, playing games, searching online, downloading, using chat rooms and emails, the forum or BBS was not very popular among the youth. The factor analysis suggested that using "Forum or BBS" plays no significant independent role for today's youth participating in society. Rather the Internet is used for entertainment /communication and practical needs. Of course we cannot exclude the possibility that entertainment and communication also contains aspects of expression of ideas and/or participation in society at large. This needs further research.

We can see that E-democracy is facing the challenges from wider access to the Internet. At least in today's China, the digital divide has hindered most youth access to expressing their views on the Internet. This marginalizes youth in developing parts of the country. We also found that forum or BBS may involve entertainment/communication and practical needs. Using "forum or BBS" is not the same as youth independently participate in society. The real participation or E-democracy would involve greater levels of information and resources, as well as training and developing special channels for youth. However the Internet is used as a channel for expressing views on society by youth and moreover it has a great potential for youth participating in society.

As I mentioned above, this study is only a piece of exploratory research. It provides some evidence of youth expression or participation through the Internet. However, because we didn't study youth forums or BBS directly, further research is needed for a greater understanding of social participation online. Quantitative surveys on youth forums or BBS and interviews would be useful for this. Also, the study suggested that future studies should include youth in rural areas and young migrants.

CHAPTER 9

The Digital North Denmark
New Ways Towards the Knowledge- and Network Society

BACKGROUND

'The Digital North Denmark' was initiated by the Danish government in 2000. North Jutland was selected to establish an IT Lighthouse to promote IT development and IT use. This means that during the project period the region of North Jutland serves as an exploratory to all Denmark by means of different projects trying new ways to prepare citizens, enterprises and public authorities for the network society. The project period runs until the end of 2003, after which time some of the projects will be concluded while others will be continued on their own.

'The Digital North Denmark' is both a vision and a very tangible entity. The vision is to create "the first network society" in the region North Jutland in Denmark. Focus is on use, dissemination and the synergy generated when deploying information technology throughout the region. 'The Digital North Denmark' contains 89 ongoing projects representing a total value of more than 80 million Euro.

THE PROJECTS

Nearly 20 mill Euro have been allocated via five project contests to 89 winning projects distributed over four main themes:

- ITBusiness- and Industrial Development
- Qualification and Education
- Digital Administration
- IT Infrastructure

The total value of the projects now amounts to 80 million Euro, one quarter is funded by the Danish Ministry of Science, Technology and Innovation.

The private industrial sector, the County of North Jutland, and the municipalities of the region cover the remaining part.

To learn more about the themes and the individual projects, please visit: www.thedigitalnorthdenmark.com .

LESSONS LEARNED

'The Digital North Denmark' is not only for the benefit of the residents of North Jutland – it is intended to make results and gain experience useful for the entire Denmark as well as other regions abroad. Therefore a really vital task for each project is to publish lessons learned, not only after the end of the project period, but also while the project is up and running. To this end project descriptions and contacts are available to the public on the website www.thedigitalnorthdenmark.com. Adding to this an extra focus is put on 'Project of the Month' and on project videos visualizing activities for different ongoing projects – also available on the website.

NEW NETWORKS

North Jutland has for a long time had good experiences with networking across professional borders and traditional fields of interest. Aalborg University has been frontrunner in the creation of networks and pioneering collaborations with especially industry and private enterprises,.

The concept of "Joint Forces Make Mutual Strength" has raised a wide range of IT-Lighthouse projects collaborating across sectors, industries and traditional geographical borders, creating new partnerships and networks. At the same time enterprises, research centers, and public institutions nationwide and abroad have become aware of the potentials of learning both from and with the IT-Lighthouse projects of North Jutland.

FOLLOW UP RESEARCH SCRUTINIZING THE IT LIGHTHOUSE

Researchers of Aalborg University are continuously monitoring the Digital North Denmark with special focus on North Jutland as a learning region. Questions researchers find interesting are among others:

- What are the specific characteristics of a learning region?
- What is the role of IT in the development of a learning region?
- In which ways is North Jutland developing into a learning region?
- Which dynamic methods for regional development have been established via the IT Lighthouse?

In practice this means that not only the individual projects, but also the IT Lighthouse of North Jutland as such will be discussed and evaluated on an ongoing basis. Helge Sander, Minister of Science, Technology and Innovation *IT is to enhance the personal freedom and the innovation of Danish society. The Digital North Denmark gives good examples of how to use partnerships between the public and the private sector to benefit the most of the potentials of IT and to deploy IT in every corner of society.*

Facts

Business and Industrial Development	21 projects worth a value of 14 million Euroare making solutions within e-business, intensive use of IT in SME's, mobile communication, bridge-building between new and old economy et cetera.
Qualification and Education	43 projects worth a value of 25 million Euro are dealing with subjects such as life-long-learning, new ways of learning and teaching, e-learning, IT for the benefit of mentally or physically disabled and with both children, young people, grown ups and elderly people as part of the target group. – Also projects creating digital art and digital communication of art and culture are here to be found.
Digital Administra-tion	21 projects worth a value of nearly 30 million Eurofocus on e-governance, e-democracy and e-health –and on increasing service levels and reducing costs.
IT Infrastruc-ture	4 projects worth a value of more than 11 million Euro focus on strategic plans for IT-infrastructure as well as interactive digital television and mobile wireless.

To learn more, please visit www.thedigitalnorthdenmark.com
Or contact us:

The Lighthouse Centre
"Brohuset"
Vesterbro 102
DK- 9000 Aalborg
Phone +45 72 14 66 81
Fax   +45 98 10 21 85
Email: fyrtaarn@nja.dk
(Now, at date of publication [late 2005], this project has concluded.
However, its aims, scope and achievements can be reviewed at the web
address above. – *Ed.)*